"If only all doctors and nurses and social workers who care for the chronically ill could read this book. If only patients and family members stricken with such losses could receive what this book can give them. While *Strange Relation* relates one illness and the life of one family, it is also, poetically, about all illnesses, all families, all struggles, all living. The art achieves the dual life of the universal and the particular, marking it as timeless, making it for us all necessary." —Rita Charon, MD, PhD, Program in Narrative Medicine, Columbia University

"Rachel Hadas's own wonderfully resonant poems, along with the rich collection of verse and prose by other writers that she weaves into her story, clarify and illuminate over and over again this thoughtful and lucid tale of love, companionship, and heartbreaking illness—illness that, as she shows us so well, is at once frighteningly alien and also deeply a part of our unavoidable vulnerability as mortal beings. Beautifully written, totally engrossing, and very sad." —Lydia Davis

"*Strange Relation* is a deeply moving, deeply personal, beautifully written exploration of how the power of grief can be met with the power of literature, and how solace can be found in the space between them." —Frank Huyler

"*Strange Relation* is a beautifully written and piercingly honest account of life with a brilliant man as he descends into dementia, in his sixties. His wife finds herself taking charge of his life: his diagnoses and treatments, his memories, his accomplishments, his day to day existence, while he withdraws into a kind of living absence and an almost total silence. Because, as she writes here, 'Even the most sympathetic doctors write no prescriptions for the imagination,' poet and scholar Rachel Hadas reveals the ways in which she has relied upon literature and poetry—some of it, poignantly, her own—as she tries to clarify each step of an uncharted and bewildering journey. This is a deeply intelligent and illuminating book, all of its many layers suffused with love." —Reeve Lindbergh

"A poignant memoir of love, creativity and human vulnerability. Rachel Hadas brings a poet's incisive eye to the labyrinth of dementia." —Danielle Ofri, MD, PhD, author of *Medicine in Translation* and *Singular Intimacies*

"Brilliant and tough-minded, poignant but clear-headed, Rachel Hadas shines a steady light on her experience as the wife of an accomplished composer who, at a comparatively early age, descended into dementia. *Strange Relation* never sacrifices truth for easy answers. Instead, Hadas uses literature to chart a course through wrenching complexities. This lauded and exceptional poet shows how language itself, the very thing her husband loses, became her shield as she crossed the ravaged lands of decision-making, making new discoveries, new friends, and new sense of the world. *Strange Relation* snaps with bravery, intelligence, and Hadas' tart, candid wisdom." —Molly Peacock

"Like an elegy, *Strange Relation* is about loss and grief. Like all elegies, it also memorializes and celebrates. Rachel Hadas, in the course of her personal narrative, cites accounts of dementia, in its social and personal meanings. She also cites works of imagination by Constantine Cavafy, Emily Dickinson, Euripides, Thom Gunn, Thomas Hardy, William Shakespeare, and many others, as well as her own poems: all integral and necessary to her subject—which ultimately is wonder at the human mind itself, in all its mysterious powers and fragilities." —Robert Pinsky

"Shakespeare writes that 'misery acquaints a man with strange bedfellows.' That misery has bedfellows never unto itself is consoling. Nonetheless, the deep kindness and intelligence of Hadas's memoir reminds us, inspiringly, not only that our bedfellow (a lover, a spouse, or misery itself) is stranger than we had thought, but that in the generosity of poetry (Merrill, Cavafy, Shakespeare, and Hadas's own) there are other keenly buoying fellowships awaiting only our awakening to them." —Michael Snediker

Strange
Relation

A MEMOIR OF MARRIAGE,
DEMENTIA, AND POETRY

Rachel Hadas

[signature]

PAUL DRY BOOKS
Philadelphia 2011

First Paul Dry Books Edition, 2011

Paul Dry Books, Inc.
Philadelphia, Pennsylvania
www.pauldrybooks.com

1 3 5 7 9 8 6 4 2
Printed in the United States of America

Library of Congress Cataloging-in-Publication Data
Hadas, Rachel.
  Strange relation : a memoir of marriage, dementia, and poetry /
Rachel Hadas. — 1st Paul Dry Books ed.
     p. cm.
  ISBN 978-1-58988-061-0 (alk. paper)
  1. Hadas, Rachel—Marriage. 2. Authors, American—20th century—
Family relationships. 3. Edwards, George, 1943—Health. 4. Dementia—
Patients—Family relationships. 5. Hadas, Rachel—Books and reading.
6. Books and reading—Psychological aspects. 7. Authorship—Psychological
aspects. 8. Literature—Philosophy. I. Title.
  PS3558.A3116Z46 2011
  811'.54—dc22
  [B]
                                                      2010039429

CONTENTS

PROLOGUE

In early 2005, my husband, George Edwards, a composer and professor of music at Columbia University, was diagnosed with dementia. He was sixty-one years old. I was fifty-six.

Neurodegenerative diseases present a field of study that is both bleak and bewildering. Starting from zero, I've learned a great deal about them in five years—enough to know how little I know, for nothing in this area of medicine is simple. Diagnoses are complicated; often only an autopsy can determine exactly which ailment the victim suffered from. Yet diagnosis, however problematic and uncertain, is more advanced than current understanding of the etiology or prevention or treatment of these diseases.

When George's dementia was first diagnosed, we were told that it was unclear whether he was suffering from Alzheimer's disease or frontotemporal dementia (FTD). At the time, I wasn't familiar with the latter term. When I investigated, I was confronted with a teeming world of names that apply to the many forms of this family of diseases. For example, frontotemporal dementia, frontotemporal lobar degeneration, and Pick's disease are three names that appear to describe the same disease. Then there is the grim alphabet soup of acronyms for different diseases in the same general family: PPA (primary progressive aphasia), CBD (corticobasal degeneration), and PSP (progressive supranuclear palsy) are three of these. All these acronyms (and there are others) refer to various neurodegenerative diseases distinct from Alzheimer's.

Two salient facts about this group of ailments—ailments of whose existence I had long been blissfully ignorant—struck me right away, since both were so clearly germane to George's case. First, these dementias tend to strike earlier in life than Alzheimer's does; the average age at onset is sixty. Looking back, George must have been about fifty-five when his illness began. Second, whereas Alzheimer's typically presents as difficulties with memory, frontotemporal dementias and their ilk tend initially to cause disturbances in language and behavior. Thus an FTD sufferer in her fifties or sixties who begins to speak less or strangely and to act withdrawn, apathetic, disorganized, disinhibited, or otherwise odd is often misdiagnosed with depression or psychosis, medicated incorrectly, or subjected to psychotherapy—which under the circumstances is an exercise in futility. George's experience fitted both these scenarios. Even now, five years along, his diagnosis isn't clear. His lumbar puncture and PET scan results are more indicative of Alzheimer's; his symptoms, at least initially, more like FTD. Some of his doctors split the difference and pronounced his illness an atypical frontal variant of Alzheimer's.

Since all these diseases are at present incurable, a precise diagnosis finally doesn't matter very much. It's equally quixotic (though perfectly natural) to hope for a clear diagnosis or for a cure. As for treatment, medication can sometimes slow down the ravages of these various dementias, although medications for Alzheimer's and FTD may not be identical (another source of confusion). Other drugs such as anti-psychotics sometimes ease symptoms like agitation. But although some dementias move faster than others, all of them are progressive. In January 2008, I moved George out of our apartment and into a dementia facility.

It's impossible to say precisely when the symptoms of George's illness began to show themselves. Just as most diagnoses of a dementia must rely on hindsight, so this book proceeds by way of several flashbacks. I wrote most of it between 2005 and 2007, years when I was living with George but in a zone of deepening silence. During those years, literature was often my most faithful companion, so this is in part a book about literature. More precisely, it's about various literatures.

There were books toward which our situation steered me that I wouldn't have read otherwise, books with eloquent titles like *Stolen Mind, Death in Slow Motion, Ambiguous Loss,* and *What If It's Not Alzheimer's?* A very different group included books and stories I had read years before and that I now saw in a new light. These included Dickens's *David Copperfield* and *Hard Times,* Wharton's *Ethan Frome,* James's *The Portrait of a Lady,* and Andersen's "The Snow Queen," among others. Greek myths, too, took on a new urgency. A situation like Agamemnon's anguished decision at Aulis or a character like the immortally decrepit Tithonus felt anything but remote; they were more like pieces of a case history. And then there was poetry. Many of the poems that sustained me during this time were pieces I'd thought I already knew. But again, they spoke to me with fresh voices—poems by Cavafy and Hardy, Dickinson and Frost, Milton and Keats, Larkin and Merrill.

Though many of them are certainly beautiful, these works of literature didn't soothe or console or lull me with their beauty. On the contrary, they made me sit up and pay attention. Each in its own way, they helped me by telling me the truth, or rather *a* truth, about the almost overwhelming situation in which I found myself. I learned what isn't always obvious under such circumstances: I wasn't alone. Other people, these works reminded me, had experienced, if not precisely my dilemma, then their own, equally hard or harder. Those people had found the courage to face and describe situations which might easily have reduced them to silence. If silence was the enemy, literature was my best friend. No matter how lonely, frightened, confused, or angry I felt, some writer had captured the sensation. How does it feel when people you thought were your friends turn away from illness? When you've almost forgotten what love is like? When you are forced to choose between unpalatable alternatives? Frost and Aeschylus and Merrill knew the answers to these questions—questions doctors don't like to ask, let alone answer. In doctors' waiting rooms or in the quiet evenings after George had gone to bed, or on the train to work, I read and read. Thank God I could still read.

And I could write. Some of the chapters in this book were written in response to my need to record a conversation, a dream, a walk, or yet another doctor's appointment. I rediscovered what every writing teacher knows, that writing what you remember helps you to remember more. Turning life at its bleakest or dullest into prose was absorbing and also rewarding; the more I wrote, the more I remembered and understood.

I'm a teacher, but first and foremost I am a poet. Since my father's death when I was seventeen years old, poetry has steadily helped me not only to express what I was feeling at a given time, but also to figure out what I was thinking. In the case of a situation as elusive and amorphous, but also as powerful and all-pervasive, as George's illness, poetry's gift of trope often shed crucial light on the prevailing gloom. What did this situation feel like? What did it resemble? How could I better wrap my mind around it? Other questions arose too: how could I mourn, or rage, or explain? How could I speak to, and sometimes for, someone who no longer spoke to me? For some people, help might well come from their faith in God. For me, help came from a source that seemed equally inexhaustible: poetry. Accordingly, some of the literature in this book consists of my own poems.

I don't want to minimize the tragedy of George's illness. It has gradually and relentlessly destroyed his mind and personality and has deprived me and our son of a husband and father we loved. No silver lining can restore George's lost brilliance to himself or to us. Nevertheless, it is true that this ordeal has eloquently reminded me of the sustaining power of literature. Part of what I hope to do in this book is to share that power.

This story, if it is a story, lacks both a clear beginning and a final resolution. Within the cloudy confines of those years when reading and writing were part of what kept me going, I tried to keep track; I tried to tell the truth. Nevertheless, it is largely a one-sided truth. Even long before his diagnosis, George had become increasingly uncommunicative. As he lost more and more language and agency, he naturally said and did less and less. Looming large in our apartment as a physical presence, he was at the same time uncannily absent, an increasingly ghostly non-presence. Much as I might like to, then, I cannot (except when I quote from his letters) record his thoughts here. I don't know what they were; and I think there were fewer and fewer of them as time went on. So although I hope to convey some of the flavor of his personality before it began to vanish, I can't claim to be telling the story from his point of view. For better or worse, this is my story.

Rachel Hadas

STRANGE RELATION

CHAPTER 1

Two Silences

The silence was the worst. Silence not as in solitude or concentration, but as in living with, eating with, waking up next to someone who has nothing to say to you. It was bleak, uncanny, sometimes infuriating, though sometimes actually peaceful: a blank slate to write on. As with nearly everything else, I got somewhat used to it, so the silence at times became almost inaudible, like background noise. But any habituation was unreliable, a chancy compromise that could suddenly collapse. Living with George's silence was a fundamental deprivation, not something it was healthy to get accustomed to. Above all, the silence was overwhelmingly, accumulatingly lonely.

Ironically, or prophetically, one of George's gifts to me almost as soon as we met was silence: shared silence. There was the silence, new to me, of sitting with him and listening to music. The silence of working together at two desks, in two rooms, even on two separate floors. The silence of reading, in the living room or in bed. The pregnant silence of thinking.

This fertile silence flourished in the country. We met in July 1976, at the MacDowell Colony in southern New Hampshire, where artists' studios, spaced out from one another in the woods to enhance the illusion of solitude, were and surely still are repositories of busy, productive silence that hums with energy. He was thirty-three. I'd never seen anyone so tall and thin. He smoked, joked (especially puns), played ping-pong and pool. He was clearly having a good time at MacDowell, yet a burning intensity, hard to describe but clear in his presence, underlay everything he did; it had to do with his height and his cheekbones, but went deeper than physique. Friendly though never chatty, funny, and apparently utterly self-sufficient, he often went back to his remote studio after dinner to compose some more. I'd never met a composer and was amazed that a whole day's work could amount to twenty-one seconds of music. I was twenty-seven and (though not yet divorced) had just recently emerged from a youthful marriage. After seven years out of school, I was going to move to Baltimore in the fall to study for my MA at the Johns Hopkins Writing Seminars. I was jittery, excited, unfocused, sleeping badly. George was about to move from Boston—where he had been teaching at the New England Conservatory, interrupted by a stint at the American Academy in Rome—to New York, where he was to join the music department at Columbia. Obviously, we were both in transition. George seemed comfortable alone, and I hadn't expected to get involved with anyone so soon after barely extricating myself from my marriage. So much for plans and expectations.

I had the sense early on that silence was George's native element. It scared me a little; I had to stretch to inhabit it. It held no terrors for him. At the time, I felt no foreboding in this knowledge. George's silence and my chatter seemed complementary, as indeed they turned out to be. Besides, he wasn't silent all the time. He had stories to tell of the two years he had recently spent at the American Academy; I had stories about my years in Greece. We talked about books—we both loved Proust—and music. At the time I met him, I recall, George was reading *The Mill on the Floss*. Sometimes I went to his studio and he played the piano for me. The apartment where he would be living in New York was in the same building where I had gone to nursery school, and so we talked about the city. There was no shortage of shared topics—it's so easy, when we're young, for paired lives to weave themselves together into an almost inextricably dense texture. Later, after his illness began, some people commented on how taciturn George had always been, as if to suggest that he hadn't really changed all that much. But back then he had been far from taciturn with me. Still, the silence behind the talk, the silence of George's intense inwardness, the way he was listening, when he composed, to something no one else could hear—this was constant, and was part of what made his personality so compelling to me from the start.

When I think of our shared pastoral silence, what comes to mind even more vividly than MacDowell in 1976 is the fall of 1980 at my family's place in Vermont. George had a Guggenheim fellowship that year; I had finished the coursework for my doctorate in comparative literature at Princeton and was trying to buckle down to writing my dissertation on landscape imagery in the poetry of Robert Frost and George Seferis. We had spent part of the summer in Vermont with my mother, who went back to the city around Labor Day to resume teaching Latin at Spence, a girls' independent school. The weather turned crisp. Apples ripened on our two apple trees and I made pies. Wearing hats and mittens, we played badminton on the lawn while fallen leaves swirled around our feet. We often ate grilled cheese and tomato sandwiches for lunch—Cabot cheese on homemade bread, late tomatoes from our garden. George called the chamber piece he was working on "Northern Spy," the name of a variety of apple and a reference to our northern sojourn.

We'd work in the morning, George upstairs, where there was a battered old upright piano that never seemed to get any more out of tune from year to year, I downstairs. The woodburning stoves on both floors kept us warm. Often in the afternoon we'd take a walk. Our favorite route was around a three-and-a-half-mile loop of dirt road that was part of a larger network of back roads through the area of Pumpkin Hill in Danville. An elegant and simple solution to the challenge of thinking while walking: we sometimes used the walk as a time of silence and solitude—I would head down the road one way and George would go the other way. We'd meet somewhere in the middle before continuing on our separate ways. Then, home again, we'd compare notes: a bird one of us had seen, or a neighbor one of us had encountered; an idea or a memory. It's hard to recall these conversations, these little reunions after the separation of our respective walks, but as Auden wrote, "though one cannot always / Remember exactly why one has been happy, / There is no forgetting that one was." That cold fall was radiant with our shared happiness.

Did George hear music as he strode along? I do know that it was on these walks that I was able to map out the shape of my thesis. Our silence was companionable, loving, full of promise. It had, now I look back on it, the suspense of a question: What was going on underneath the surface? What would the silence give birth to? The surface of the silence was tranquil; its depths were rich with something mysterious.

The silence that came increasingly to reign in our house as George gradually changed from one person into another beginning in the late 1990s was neither productive nor companionable. It was bleak and empty, and it never led to anything except more of itself.

My poem "Two Silences" contrasts the earlier kind of silence—the silence I encountered when I met George in 1976, and which was such a crucial component of the joyful autumn we spent in Vermont in 1980—with this later kind, which ever so slowly and stealthily, when no one was expecting such a thing to happen, when no one was on the alert for the transformation, took the first silence's place.

Two Silences

Not the full silence of a sun-warmed furrow,
countless minute processes at work
tunneling, ramifying, reaching out;
intentions, connections, and adjustments:
    make a note; look up;
smile; meet an eye; then turn back to the task,
the blessing of the sun, the heat of thought,

but empty silence. Intermittent wind
sighs around the corner of a crumbling
    stucco wall that straggles
between the last few houses and a sea
    no color; a horizon
where past and future in one flat line meet,
gaze a diluted blue, lips firmly shut.

CHAPTER 2

In Your Chair

When did this empty silence begin? When did the illness begin? The two questions are the same, really—one to which I keep doggedly returning, although it is not a question that can be answered. I do know that sometime around 2000 I had a dream. I remember the dream because I wrote a poem recording it—a poem whose date I can more or less place because it was published in 2002. My dreams often generate poems, which in turn, in however coded or hermetic a way, commemorate the dreams that gave rise to them.

But my dreams do more than engender poems. They also tell me things my waking mind doesn't know, probably because it doesn't want to know them. Looking back at the last seven lines of this little poem, whose title is "In Your Chair," I can now see the first signs that I was beginning, in some subliminal realm, to register that there was something wrong with my husband. Subtle as these signs are in the poem, I recognize them now with clarity. Here are the lines:

> You were sitting in your armchair
> Surrounded, almost submerged, by drifts of paper—
> Mail, piles of it, and almost all for me.
> The heap seemed festive, Christmas-lavish, wasteful.
> I fished a letter out almost at random,
> Then scurried to the atlas, found the map
> So I could show you where I would be going.

So much of what would happen, of what had slyly already begun to happen, is here. George, who had always had abundant physical energy—what used to be called "animal spirits"—is depicted immobile in his chair. This is an accurate reflection of the fact that he had indeed (when?) begun to spend more and more time sitting down doing nothing in particular. I am seen scurrying to and fro, bringing bits of the world to him—a world that has arrived in the mail for me, a world mapped out for my future travels, travels on which only "I would be going."

None of this was obvious to me when I wrote the poem. I only recall vaguely realizing that "In Your Chair" bore a bleak resemblance to what our lives had become. It's hard to say whether the prescience of the dream or my own cluelessness is more striking. I had written my as yet unacknowledged intuition into the poem, which I cheerfully submitted for publication. "In Your Chair" appeared in the *New Republic*, June 3, 2002. I have no idea what, if anything, the poem meant to anyone who read it. "In Your Chair" was collected in my 2004 volume of poetry, *Laws*, but again its footprint was light. My little poem sank, as the vast majority of poems do, into an appropriate obscurity. I myself almost forgot it. But the poem, like the dream, has an ominous resonance for me now.

The dream was a portal to the lonely, chilly place our marriage had for some time been turning into—or perhaps less a portal than an isolated marker, a small beacon in a place of slowly gathering shadows. Even though the dream was only rescued from oblivion by my poem, it seems more vivid now than the years from about 1999 to 2004, which were shadowy and confusing, painful and tiring, but still close enough to normal that nothing much stands out. All my insights appear to have played out at the subliminal level of dreams.

George and I both had teaching jobs, he at Columbia, I at Rutgers. He still played the piano before dinner, still read *La*

Gazzetta dello Sport on Sunday mornings. Our son began his final year in high school in the fall of 2001, and there were college applications to be seen to. That George had nothing to do with these I took for granted; ever since he had been chair of Columbia's music department, from 1996 to 1999, I had taken over pretty much everything on the domestic front, from shopping and cooking to college applications. The fall of 2001 was also the first time Jon had a serious girlfriend. Her sixteenth birthday fell on September 11.

A huge public event trumps private trouble, especially trouble as amorphous as ours. No one forgets 9/11, but much in the next few years has now receded to a dull blur for me. These years offered a few, a very few, happy events, such as our son's graduation from high school. Sharing our empty nest felt uneventful, quiet . . . too quiet. Our lives grew more and more separate. In the spring of 2003, I went to St. Louis to see my half-brother, who was ill, being celebrated by his colleagues in the English department at Washington University. This occasion was a Hadas family reunion of sorts, but I knew George wouldn't want to come and I didn't ask him. Early in 2004, I went to visit David for the last time. When I was preparing to leave for the airport, George didn't say goodbye, didn't carry my suitcase to the door. He stood in the living room like—I remember thinking—a tree in a yard. I got back home from the trip late, about midnight, to find the door chained. George was asleep, and it was almost impossible to wake him up; when he did get up and let me in, he was furious.

To think about this behavior was to be angry and frightened. Somehow managing not to think about it, at least not on the surface, I trudged on. George's stays at the Virginia Center for the Creative Arts in 2003 and in 2004 postponed the moment of truth. Certainly his sabbatical in the academic year 2003–04 deferred the inevitable day when it became manifestly clear he couldn't teach any more. I remember feeling lonely during the weeks of his absences, but then in his presence I also felt lonely. His letters (in 2003? Was he still writing letters in 2004?) were skeletally short.

In March 2004, a Columbia colleague of George's, a man who had known him for many years, bravely visited and told me that people in the department were worried about George's behavior. I remember I cried. I didn't deny that something was wrong, but the colleague was looking in the wrong direction ("Is he depressed? Is he drinking?"), and I didn't know where to look either.

During these years, we went to Vermont in the summers as usual. George spent a lot of time stirring the compost heap or sitting on the porch in a rocking chair smoking cigarettes. He drove very little, didn't go shopping. He played the piano, some, on the rickety upright. I remember silently willing him to go upstairs and compose. For many years, from the time we met in 1976 until sometime in the late nineties, George's power of concentration—a power I envied—had had the almost palpable aura of a force field. What had happened to that fierce focus? Now he would go upstairs to the piano and compose for a few minutes before coming back down and wandering out to the garden to stir the compost heap again. Skin rashes—a recurring problem—became increasingly intractable: George was itchy, uncomfortable. We saw a New York dermatologist in 2003 and 2004, and she prescribed a range of medications that I remember included both antihistamines and cortisone. Dulled, exhausted, itchy, not complaining, not explaining, miserable, confused, George plodded on. All this I see clearly only now.

Fall 2004. Jon was a junior at Swarthmore, planning to go to India for his spring term. George had resumed teaching at Columbia—except that his teaching wasn't going at all well. Sometime early in the semester, another colleague of his emailed to let me know that people in the music department were all very worried about George. I've already had that conversation, I replied snippily. The weeks went by. George visited the dermatologist once or twice more, with no discernible improvement. And the semester staggered on until December.

At this point some of the fog clears. The confusion in which we were struggling was no less thick, but I became able to see it. From vague and flat, my memories from here on become much sharper. To convey that sharpness, I narrate scenes that remain especially vivid, such as a pivotal visit to a doctor, in the present tense.

CHAPTER 3

Into the Murky World

"What year did you get married?"

A gray December morning, 2004. George and I are sitting side by side, facing his new doctor across the desk. The internist Dr. L, a fresh-faced man with prematurely white hair, seems somehow able to simultaneously look us both in the eye, ask George questions, and type into his computer. I have accompanied George—brought him here, really—and asked to come into the doctor's office with him. Did I already know that he wouldn't be able to navigate by himself—navigate getting to a new place, navigate the history, navigate the Q and A?

George hesitates. At what point (I ask myself now) did I get so accustomed to his hesitant speech, as if he's rummaging around for reluctant answers? Exactly when did I get used to answering for him? And how could I have assumed for so long that in the fast-paced back and forth of the classroom, he must somehow be functioning just fine, although at home he barely spoke? All such assumptions, flimsy but stubborn, had collapsed like a house of cards the week before, when George's chair at the Columbia music department telephoned me in the middle of the day and the whole story came out—missed appointments, puzzled and frustrated students lining up to complain. "He can't teach," she said. I was appalled—she and I both cried on the phone—but I was not surprised. A doctor had to be found to sign off on a medical leave. So here we are.

George hasn't yet answered Dr. L's question. Asking what year we were married is, I suppose, part of taking a history. Or is it more like a memory test? Or maybe both? At some point in the silence, I reluctantly recognize that, whatever the reason for this question, George has no idea of the answer.

A few snowflakes tumble lazily through the slice of gray sky I can glimpse out the window behind Dr. L. On the wall behind his computer are photographs of his family: laughing boys, a pretty woman, a dog. I drink some water. I'm not thirsty. Hot coffee would taste a lot better than cold water, but the bottle of water keeps me busy. I fold my hands around it and look down, or raise it to my lips to plug myself up. Clearly, I am not supposed to supply the answer to this question.

"1990?" George says, with a rising inflection that turns the answer into a guess.

I no longer remember precisely what happened next. Did I look at him? Did the doctor look at me? I know I went on clutching my water bottle like a talisman. I don't think I said in so many words—to either of those tall, handsome men, the one across the desk typing and the one next to me, the one to whom I'd been married since 1978—that 1990 was not the answer. I do remember that rising inside me during this whole long, long appointment was a feeling it is a little too melodramatic to call panic. It was, rather, a sharply etched loneliness— a loneliness that stepped out from the shadows to which I had so far consigned it right onto center stage. There was also a queasy sense of shifting: shifting of power, of paradigms, of alliances, of allegiances. The center wasn't holding, and I was in the process, as I hung on to my clammy water bottle for dear life, of casting about for a new center. In all this there was alarm and fear, but really, as I now recall it, no surprise.

Two other bits of the Q and A stick with me from that first morning when I fully entered the world of what I had not yet learned to call "dementia." At some point in the history, or interview, or interrogation, Dr. L asked George to take what I now know is a standard memory quiz: remember three words for ten minutes or so. I can still repeat them: dog, pencil, car. George remembered none of them.

Toward the end of the session, Dr. L asked George about his hobbies, what he did for fun. Tennis, chess, and reading, came the answer. With a chill that had already become familiar, I realized that George no longer played chess, barely read, and for the past few summers had played tennis only when I or our son spent an hour on the court with him in Vermont.

Soon, very soon, I would learn (although for several years I still lapsed occasionally) not to share my thoughts about my husband with my husband. But that morning, when the appointment was finally over and the prescriptions and referrals were in my bag, when we were once more in the corridor outside the doctor's office, I thoughtlessly turned to George and said, "You know, what you said to the doctor about your hobbies—you don't really play tennis or chess or read much any more, so it wasn't really accurate."

Why would I say something so hurtful? Because for twenty-five years I had been used to sharing my thoughts with him; because I still habitually turned to him as a reality check, hoping he'd be able to comfort me, to brush away my silly misgivings. Because I desperately wanted to be reassured, and for years he had been pretty good at reassuring me. I was behaving as if he knew the truth of his own condition and as if that truth was, as he said to the neurologist we saw a few weeks later, that he was functioning at ninety percent of capacity. But what I blurted out was wounding, and he blamed the messenger. All I remember of his response are the four words "You make me angry."

I didn't look ahead then—the present was more than enough to cope with. But I now see, and I'm pretty sure I had an inkling even that winter morning, that I was moving rapidly into a bleak new zone where my relationship with my husband could no longer be the natural center of gravity. Indeed I was well ensconced in that zone already, and had been for some time, but only now, like the characters in Sartre's *No Exit* settling into their overheated room, was I taking stock of my surroundings.

Already in December 2004, my role was to serve as an interpreter or translator between George and the world. This task involved much more than answering doctors' questions. I had become the guardian not only of George's medical history but also of the story of his life, a story that was increasingly difficult for him to articulate and of which it seemed that I alone knew many of the facts. Experiences, feelings, all kinds of memories from six decades of lived life—somehow all this had come into my keeping. George hadn't been close to his siblings for years; his mother, disabled since 1979, had died in 2001. Colleagues? Friends? Where were they? Our son and I were the only people at this point who really seemed to know him, and Jonathan, who had been only fourteen or so when his father began to change, was now away at college. I was the sole custodian of the fragile freight of George's past. It was a lonely role.

CHAPTER 4

Something That Went Before

The visit to Dr. L's office at the end of 2004 served as a threshold. We'd crossed over from the world of routine, however specious and brittle, to the cloudy realm of dementia. In that realm, I continued to seek a clarity that I slowly learned was not available. But as I paced the cage-like confines of this place, one striking thing did emerge, something I should have known but had never thought about: other people had been here before. Many had left startlingly clear and eloquent accounts of their sojourns in this realm.

I had never heard the term frontotemporal dementia (FTD) before January 2005 when the first neurologist we consulted gave the ambiguous diagnosis: AD (Alzheimer's disease) or FTD. Soon, I was reading books about it, and in September 2006, I took myself to an FTD conference in San Francisco and learned more. This was not a quest for a cure; I had no hope of that. These diseases are not curable. Still, I wanted to know more, and I wanted to do what I could—if not for George, then for myself. If I could even begin to wrap my mind around the spooky condition that was changing our lives—that had been changing them for quite a few years already—I would be able to reclaim some sense of agency. The awful sleepwalking quality that marks my memory of the years leading up to 2005 was dispelled.

Some of the books I read about dementia offered a welcome validation of my own experience. In particular, when the writers touched on the sneaky onset of these diseases, I often wanted to write "Yes!" in the margin.

Here is Lawrence Shainberg in *Memories of Amnesia*:

> Brain damage isn't always as grotesque as normal brains expect it to be. It's true that it can strike like a hurricane, but sometimes it's more like a gentle breeze, a subtle change of vectors that leaves you headed not in the opposite direction, but almost exactly where you were headed before.

Shainberg's useful insight is that instead of changing radically, someone in the early stages of a neurodegenerative disease may simply seem to be more pronouncedly themselves, or different only in some trivial respect. A case in point: George had always been somewhat quiet and withdrawn, so his gradually becoming more quiet and withdrawn didn't seem cause for alarm.

In *Losing Lou-Ann*, an account of his wife's illness with Pick's disease (one name for FTD, which is a confusing umbrella term), Clinton Erb uses a word that frequently appears in the medical literature, with good reason: insidious.

> [Pick's disease] is an insidious disease. You don't know when it starts, and by the time you're aware of its presence, it has already had a major effect, profoundly changing the person you knew. Little things happened that could be easily explained by other reasons. Even looking back, it is hard to determine when the first signs began to appear.

This is absolutely right, and Erb goes on to make a subtler point I have also found helpful:

> No one's life is seen whole by any individual. All those who know the person see a part, and each person then develops his or her own individual interpretation of the unusual behaviors. Each person who knew or interacted with Lou-Ann

saw behaviors that were abnormal. No one saw the whole of her life, so the full extent of her actions were not known to any one person.

George's students and colleagues, for example, all saw changes in his behavior, but it took about four years for them to get on the same page. I experienced his increasing coldness and passivity, but I resolutely shut my eyes or looked the other way. As Erb puts it, I developed my own individual interpretation of the unusual behaviors. George was stressed out from serving as chair of Columbia's music department. He was annoyed by our teenage son's loud playing of his electric guitar. His skin problems, and the attendant medications, were getting him down.

Not the least confusing feature of this maddening family of diseases is that all such interpretations probably contain a grain of truth. There is also the habituation factor; things change so slowly that family members don't notice. Nancy Mairs puts it this way in *Waist-High in the World*, an account of her life with multiple sclerosis:

> There were . . . signs to be explained or ignored . . . [the illness] developed so slowly that people who had known me for a long time grew used to it, and those who had just met me assumed I'd always had it. Some must have wondered about it but been too "polite" to mention it. Our society promotes a kind of magical thinking, whereby some personal peculiarities, especially those implying dysfunction, can be effaced through studied inattention.

Live with someone long enough, and you don't really need to try very hard to be inattentive.

Yet sooner or later spouses do notice a change. Or perhaps it would be truer to say that, at some point, we begin to notice that we haven't been noticing. In a brave account that deserves to be better known, *Stolen Mind: The Slow Disappearance of Ray Doernberg*—a book whose margins I found myself marking copiously because I recognized so much that it described—Myrna Doernberg's very vagueness bears eloquent testimony to the elusiveness of the early symptoms:

> When did things change? What were the signs? Less initiative perhaps, some loss of interest . . . He seemed discontent, less involved. We thought it temporary, a response to life changes.

The "response to life changes" is also noted by Clinton Erb and Nancy Mairs. I myself had wondered whether George was having a midlife crisis—an explanation the Doernbergs also tried on for size. Myrna Doernberg continues:

> [T]here had been a change in Ray . . . He was reading very little. He was quieter and less involved socially, lacked a certain zest for life, and didn't seem as involved in work . . . Ray had become increasingly quiet, generally passive in his response to life. He hardly ever spoke or seemed interested in anything. We had always been able to share everything; it was a relationship I cherished and knew was rare and special. We were best friends. But now I felt alone. He seemed unconcerned about what was happening in his and our life . . . gradually Ray had relinquished more and more decision-making and responsibility to me. What did all this mean? What was happening?

Yes, I thought when I read this, yes to the reading very little, the passivity, the relinquishing of decision-making. Yes to the disengagement. Yes to Myrna Doernberg's poignantly expressed bewilderment and to the apt phrase in her subtitle, "slow disappearance."

One theme that emerges over and over is that if the "disappearance" of the ill person is slow, then this indolent pace (as our first neurologist phrased it) is often matched by the slowness of the sufferer's family to see, to understand, to acknowledge. Indeed, once family members do finally see, they often feel compelled to write about the revelation, not so much to spread the news, I think, as to garner the additional measure of understanding that writing provides. I know this is true of me.

What's going on in other people's minds is notoriously hard to fathom. Only in fiction, perhaps, is it possible to see into another person's mind, to comprehend them wholly—but possible only for the author, not the characters. Even in fiction, characters who think they understand other people are often groping in a mist. Fiction can give us a clear picture of the confusion that human beings so often experience when their assumptions turn out to be erroneous, when their expectations clash with reality. My reading of fiction and poetry was inevitably colored by living alongside George's illness; I was often startled to be reminded of some of my experiences by passages not only in memoirs about dementia but also in novels about very different topics.

One of the best depictions I know of the imperceptibly stealthy advance of unwelcome knowledge is to be found not in a book about Alzheimer's or FTD but in a little-known 2006 novel by the British writer Barry Unsworth. In a pivotal scene in Unsworth's *The Ruby in Her Navel*, the amiable but gullible narrator gradually arrives at the realization that he has been duped. The description of the almost imperceptible growth of his suspicions also applies to the slow realizations I've already considered of spousal illness. In the novel, the issue isn't a previously unrecognized or unacknowledged dementia, but the previously unrecognized or unacknowledged treachery of the narrator's beloved. Nevertheless the principle holds:

> When the first specter of doubt appeared I do not know. It did not come as a shaft or sudden visitation but like a companion that had been walking by my side, unnoticed, for a time I could not determine. Through the hours of that first afternoon and those of the next day and the next . . . all the time he had been there, this companion.

Of course the realization in this case takes only a few days, not years, but how beautifully Unsworth captures the subtle transition between not suspecting that anything is wrong and knowing that something is. I'm reminded of Mary Shelley's comment, in her recollection of how *Frankenstein* came to be written, that "Every thing must have a beginning . . . and that beginning must be linked to something that went before."

That elusive "something that went before" finds an echo in Jonathan Franzen's reference to "invisibility" in his essay "My Father's Brain." Franzen describes his father's tendency not to do very much, even before the onset of his illness (though the unanswerable question of when the illness actually began inevitably rears its head). Hence

> the sameness of [my father's] days tended to make him invisible to me. From the early years of his mental decline I can dredge up exactly one direct memory: watching him . . . struggle and fail to calculate the tip of a restaurant bill.

When I read this passage, I did more than nod in comprehension and mark the margin of the page; I found that I had an almost identical memory. Early in the fall of 2004, my nephew Edward was visiting from London, and he, George, and I went out to a restaurant for lunch. George paid with his credit card, but when the bill came he obviously had no idea not only how to calculate the tip but even where to sign the receipt. I also remember that when we three had breakfast the next day at the corner diner, George said nothing—not one word.

Another useful observation of Franzen's corresponds to Clinton Erb's point that no one person ever sees anyone else's behavior as a whole. Franzen writes:

> One of the basic features of the mind is its keenness to construct wholes out of fragmentary parts. We all have a literal blind spot in our vision where the optic nerve attaches to the retina, but our brain unfailingly registers a seamless world around us. We catch part of a word and hear the whole . . . I

think I was inclined to interpolate across my father's silences and mental absences and to persist in seeing him as the same old wholly whole Earl Franzen. I still needed him to be an actor in my story of myself.

And if a grown son living far away needs an aging parent to be such an actor, consider the greater need of a husband or wife whose partner of perhaps decades is slowly vanishing before his or her eyes.

CHAPTER 5

And Choices Disappear

When we were given George's approximate diagnosis in January 2005, I felt trapped in a situation I hadn't asked to be in. Struggling against that situation or accepting it seemed equally useless and demoralizing. Assimilating the news intellectually wasn't the problem, but digesting it emotionally felt like being asked to swallow a large reptile in one gulp. (Or was it the reptile swallowing me?) If I could take the news in at all, I could only do it little by little, and I'd have to do it in my own way.

Just as I found that the books I was reading helped to capture and express the isolation I felt, I also found help from another source—Greek mythology. When it comes to no-win situations, mythology furnishes what it is no exaggeration to call classic examples of indigestible choices. Doctors don't like to use the word tragedy, but myths bring tragic concepts to life. Think of Agamemnon faced with the alternatives of disbanding the army and slinking home or sacrificing his daughter. "Which of these is without evils?" he asks, according to the Chorus in Aeschylus's *Agamemnon*. But then somewhere in the process of agonizing, he dons what Richmond Lattimore translates as "the yoke of necessity." He hardens his mind and does what he thinks needs to be done. My poem "Choice" comments on this dilemma.

Choice

In the majestic opening choral ode
of *Agamemnon*, when the moment came,
what garment did the general put on?
Necessity. He wore it like a yoke,

the chorus sing. Thenceforth there could be no
turning back. To sacrifice his daughter
or leave the navy stranded by the water?
The yoke was heavy. What he did, we know.

Mythology not only provides analogues but also reminds us how much easier our lot is than that of the tragic hero. No one's life was at stake in my situation. All I had to do was decide how to deal with a situation I couldn't change. In other words, the only choice I faced was the choice of my own attitude. But the very limitedness of that choice—the fact that all that remained to me was the Buddhist or Stoic choice of how I'd respond to an illness that would inevitably shape the rest of our lives—felt for a while almost unbearably harsh, and I did my share of thrashing and flailing. If there was any room at all in which to maneuver, it felt fearfully narrow.

But that narrow space allowed room enough to ponder not only the notion of choice but other concepts that suddenly, in this new setting, seemed germane—concepts like duty, whose fusty Victorian flavor ("For duty, duty must be done, / The rule applies to everyone," as Gilbert and Sullivan remind us) was, in light of my new life, changing into something different.

Wiggle Room

"Obligation" is a rainy word,
out of date and dowdy and austere
as "duty," unexpectedly severe,
and hardly ever, these past decades, heard

unless after the fact, to glue a label
on what preceded. Late, the realization:
do what you have to. Choice is not an option.
With little room, you cope as you are able.

That little room, that wiggle room, allows
at least a nod or headshake. Yes or no:
landscapes you discover as you go,
prairie, valley, swamp, a stand of trees

where darkness yields surprisingly to dawn
in the mind's sky a hundred times a day.
Morning and evening, the old Q and A.
What should I wear? Oh, obligation.

Poems get to eat their cake and have it too. This poem of
mine suggests both that one does get used to the new choice-
less landscape of obligation and that, as one gets used to it, a
little space of freedom appears. Why shouldn't both be true?
For poems afford us the privilege of what James Merrill called
double-entry bookkeeping: two layers of meaning with each
image.

Continuing to struggle with and within the new and different landscape of my life, I came to understand tragedy as I
never had before: from the inside. The yoke of necessity that
Agamemnon put on seemed to bear down on me, for example,
whenever I got off a plane. If flying out of town meant rising
above the landscape of my life, then returning meant reenter-
ing the terrain of struggle.

Deplaning

To leave the city, the apartment; stray
from the well-worn track where no one speaks
for half a day, a day, a week, two weeks,
bestows perspective, I was going to say,

as if absence were coterminous
with distance. As if I were on a plane
rising above the daily, the mundane.
As if flying cut me wholly loose.

Thinking clearly is so hard to do!
Do I mean pondering my situation
resembles flying? Or that aviation
opens the window for a better view?

Up in the air, this is all I can see:
little earthy patches, green and brown;
meandering rivers gleaming in the sun;
then fields of billowing cloud, then simply sky.

A bump, and we return to gravity.
I unbuckle simile, deplane,
trudge out into terrestrial life again,
that hazy realm where every boundary—

so sharp seen from the vantage of the air—
melts into mist. Cloaked like conspirators,
responsibilities, routines, and chores
beckon afresh, and choices disappear.

It's not only that coming back down to earth puts a crimp
in one's escapist fantasies. As George's illness progressed, future
possibilities that I (and perhaps he) had taken for granted, pleasant choices that had seemed to ramify like woodland paths,
faded away. What choices? The options were fewer and fewer.

CHAPTER 6

In Telling Fearful News

Digesting the news of a diagnosis is possible, given time. But how to tell the news to other people? Do they really want to know? And assuming they do, does one behave with compassion and break the news gently? Or does one pass along the harsh blow one has been dealt?

Such issues evaporate over time. But they loomed unreasonably large for me during the lonely early months of 2005, when George's diagnosis was new and I was on sabbatical, with plenty of time to brood. In February of that year (this is embarrassing to remember), I wrote a letter to some of our friends and some of George's colleagues informing them of his diagnosis. I used the term I'd just learned, frontotemporal dementia. I tried to maintain a relatively upbeat tone. Perhaps because the name of the disease was as unfamiliar to the letter's recipients as it had been to me, the news I was trying to convey gently didn't seem to register. Besides, how would anyone answer such a letter?

Over the succeeding years, countless individual conversations have more or less accomplished the task my letter failed at. Since George's diagnosis remains somewhat unclear, I no longer try to explain it in detail. But at the time, the challenge of communicating with the outside world seemed as gnarly as the challenge of talking to the increasingly silent man I was living with.

The inscrutable diagnosis went in and out of focus in my own thinking. After all, I asked myself, was relative clarity not better than no clarity at all? In the spring of 2005, the stronger light, no matter what blemishes it revealed, seemed like a good omen—though of what I didn't know.

Diagnosis

I turn the diagnosis in my mind.
Sometimes it fills me, more than fills me, stretches
down to my toes and fingers, sometimes shrinks
to a nubbin I forget is there.
Sometimes it casts a lurid light on every sallow hour.

Yet when at other times the same beam falls
on any little dingy fact, a window
opens onto a world
marked, marred, scarred, but also rinsed clean,
radiant in the light of early spring.

Small individual decisions about whom to tell, what to tell, and how, kept cropping up that spring. A humble household object can help bring things into focus, and I found myself remembering a holiday gift that a colleague had given me at the end of 2004—a gift I hadn't been enthusiastic about at the time, but that now seemed suggestive.

The Coaster

It seemed the classic useless Christmas present,
something I never would have bought myself:
a boxed set of four small square beige fringed coasters
handwoven of Irish linen.

Lo and behold, a buffer, an absorber
turned out to be exactly what I needed
to blot spilled tea, to keep a steaming mug
from making a ring on the desk.

In telling fearful news, there are at least
two choices: splash it out or pour it gently
into a waiting cup
resting on a coaster—better way

and worse, and it is possible, it is
crucial and inevitable: choose.

I didn't always want to pour the news out gently, though. At the receiving end it had been painful; I was tempted to pass the pain along. But then, as in the hapless letter I'd written, I would discover in myself the impulse to comfort people to whom I had just uttered some direful phrase containing the word "dementia," as if I were carrying around dressings to apply to wounds I myself had inflicted—but had inflicted only because these wounds had already been inflicted on me. The situation was symmetrical; it was also convoluted, paradoxical, and merciless.

Two other poems from this period also grapple with the shape-shifting dilemma of telling the bad news. I accepted an invitation to dinner from a sympathetic friend, only to realize I wouldn't be able to face her sympathy. I broke the date.

Broken Date, Ledge, Bare Floor

I break my dinner date.
It suddenly feels unbearable to narrate
the horrid history. Nuanced sympathy,
gentle wisdom—I wave them both away.

And yet another day
it seems intolerable not to tell.
I totter between twin impossibilities,
perch on a ledge precarious and cold

yet offering space to breathe.
I venture back indoors:

Someone seems to have taken up the rugs,
revealing the grain of the wood
on bare and polished floors.

The twin impossibilities of "Broken Date" also animate
my poem "Push Me Pull You," which touches upon the contagious nature of the aggressive impulses that hover largely
unacknowledged around the communicating of bad news.
Contagious, I mean, to the recipient of the news, who may
then wish (at least this was my experience) to pass the aggres-
sion on, to lob it back. You're asking me? I felt. Okay, I'll tell
you. But it won't be pretty.

Push Me Pull You

The truth went through me like a spear.
And as I had been punctured,
I wanted to puncture others.
I wanted to spread the pain
and then to poultice it,
to flash my wounds, then hide them.

My spears were words
and words had always been my friends
so I thought I could wield them like weapons.
But they snaked in my hands and turned and hissed and bit.
Are all sharp things so double-edged, so shifty?
Are all live things so sharp?

My father used to call a pencil
sharpened at both ends a Pushme Pullyou,
which I envisioned as an animal
skinny, slightly comical, but scary.
Patted and stroked in either direction,
it could turn on you and bare its little teeth.

CHAPTER 7

Readings in the Kingdom of Illness

1

In the spring semester of 2005, I happened to be on sabbatical, but I probably would have had to take a leave anyway. There was a lot to be seen to—more doctors, more tests: George had an MRI, a CT scan, and a PET scan. He had neuropsychological tests (in which he placed in the first percentile in some categories). His skin problems worsened; rashes over much of his body itched and oozed, so that our sheets were damp and smelly every morning. He scratched in his sleep. He sometimes slept fourteen hours a day or more. When he was awake, he drifted silently through the apartment like a ghostly clown, in the red and blue pajama-like occlusion suit one dermatologist had recommended—a sort of synthetic envelope designed to keep ointments from staining the sheets, or to maintain body humidity, or something. (Like frontotemporal dementia, "occlusion suit" was a new term in my vocabulary, unwelcome but unforgettable.) Our medicine cabinet and bedside table filled with sticky ointments. One of George's chief occupations was what he called anointing himself. It never seemed to do much good.

Our son was in India for the spring of his junior year. He had offered to stay home, but there didn't seem to be much point in sacrificing his semester abroad. His flight in mid-January fell between the PET scan and the results, which proved unsurprising but also noncommittal: "abnormal PET scan most consistent with Alzheimer's disease," read the printout. There was hypoperfusion (reduced blood flow) in the frontal, temporal, and parietal lobes, bilaterally—pretty much everywhere in George's brain.

In addition to doctors' appointments, there was paperwork: applications for Social Security disability, consultations with the (Kafkaesque term) privacy officer at Columbia's human resources department. George couldn't make phone calls, give a history, ask or answer questions, or remember what was said to him, so I had a lot of talking and listening to do. There were taxi and subway trips, and there was time, plenty of time, in waiting rooms. I tried to have, at all times, a book to read and a notebook to write in.

The books I was reading for the first time that spring were mostly about dementia. But I was doing a lot of rereading too, much of it poetry. For the first time I understood the title of one of my father's books, *Old Wine, New Bottles*. What I was reading wasn't new; the context was, and that new context informed the reading. Allegra Goodman writes in an essay called "Pemberley Previsited":

> I think unfolding is what rereading is about. Like pleated fabric, the text reveals different parts of its pattern at different times. And yet every time the text unfolds, in the library, or in bed, or upon the grass, the reader adds new wrinkles. Memory and experience press themselves into each reading so that each encounter informs the next.

Poems reopened for me that spring in a harshly new context, for after a prolonged gray period, George had fully entered what Susan Sontag and others have called the kingdom of illness, and I was right there next to him. "In a sense," writes Flannery O'Connor, "sickness is a place, more instructive than a long trip to Europe, and it's always a place where there's no company, where nobody can follow." A spouse, however, can't help following. The poet Donald Hall writes of his wife's illness that "our only address was leukemia." Our.

How does it feel to live at such an address? Everyone's experience of illness is different, but certain features I came to know in my capacity as spouse or escort or traveling companion are probably pretty common. The kingdom of chronic illness is a realm of contradictions, at once cluttered and empty. Time races and crawls. Boredom and despair take turns sticking out their tongues at you. (I was going to write "hope and fear," but although I hoped George's skin problems would one day be diagnosed and cured, I never had any hope that such a thing was possible with his dementia.) A crushing sameness prevails: the loneliness of the place where, in O'Connor's words, nobody can follow. Doctors apart, where is everybody? What has happened?

Later on, when I began to join support groups, the isolation lessened, but early in 2005 its weight felt crushing. And yet living with a sick person doesn't stop the caregiver from leading his or her own life at the same time. Instead, what the poet Molly Peacock calls the double track begins. I was still a professor, though my being on leave enhanced the loneliness of this time. I was still a poet. I was still a reader. In the deepening silence of my life with George, I found that I could hear poems more clearly. Indeed, I found that poems were among my most faithful friends. They made no promises they couldn't keep; they didn't avoid me; they didn't ask unanswerable questions. They were wise—wise not because they wanted to refer us to a new dermatologist but because they turned out to understand and express the truth of our situation.

Some of the poems I was rereading, as they unfolded themselves for me afresh, expressed abandonment, anger, puzzlement with far more eloquence and conviction than I could have mustered on my own. Here is the wife in Frost's "Home Burial" on the behavior of the bereaved couple's friends:

> "The nearest friends can go
> With anyone to death, comes so far short
> They might as well not try to go at all.
> No, from the time when one is sick to death,
> One is alone, and he dies more alone.
> Friends make pretence of following to the grave,
> But before one is in it, their minds are turned
> And making the best of their way back to life
> And living people, and things they understand."

Having delivered these deadly nine lines, the woman changes her tone. She loses her cool and goes on to rail, however briefly, at the behavior she's just finished calmly describing: "'But the world's evil. I won't have grief so / If I can change it. Oh, I won't. I won't!'" *If* I can change it. The kingdom of illness gives some gifts; it bestows an alarming clarity on the way those inside it view those outside. But it does not give insiders the power to change anyone's behavior.

Turning away from illness or death is one natural human response, though of course not the only one. Friends can appear from the most unexpected quarters; doctors professionally but often also generously turn toward, not away from illness. But there's a kind of turning different from either the cold shoulder or the offer of help. I mean the kind of apostrophic turning to address superhuman agents, which is not only a salient human impulse in times of trouble but also a crucial poetic move. The isolation and suffering that illness brings provide an especially rich environment for the apostrophic gesture in poetry—the temptation to turn to some powerful interlocutor, often in order to pose a question.

The questions we ask when we're in trouble usually contain the unhelpful word or idea "why," and they usually go unanswered. James Merrill, enumerating the incidents of "one's household opera" in his poem "Matinees," describes the apostrophic gesture in theatrical terms:

> The quick darkening
> In which a prostrate figure must inquire
> With every earmark of its being meant
> Why God in Heaven harries him/her so.

Even allowing for Merrill's tongue in cheek, pain comes through here. The gesture may be conventional and histrionic, but the suffering is genuine. A rawer instance of that unanswerable "why" can be found in Lear's anguished question over the body of Cordelia: "Why should a dog, a horse, a rat have life, / And thou no life at all?" Even in its agony, the question is rhetorical. Lear doesn't expect an answer.

A poem I read for the first time in that difficult spring of 2005 takes the anguished "why" for granted and attempts instead to provide some sort of explanation. Its strategy is to give voice to the forces many questioners probably barely envision. "The Subalterns," one of many Thomas Hardy poems I had previously known only by title, is quoted in full in Donald Davie's study of Hardy, which I plucked off a shelf in a friend's guestroom. Since I had never read the poem before, memory didn't figure in my response to "The Subalterns," but experience most certainly did.

I

> "Poor wanderer," said the leaden sky,
>   "I fain would lighten thee,
> But there are laws in force on high
>   Which say it must not be."

II

> "I would not freeze thee, shorn one," cried
>   The North, "knew I but how
> To warm my breath, to slack my stride;
>   But I am ruled as thou."

III

"To-morrow I attack thee, wight,"
    Said Sickness. "Yet I swear
I bear thy little ark no spite,
    But am bid enter there."

IV

"Come hither, Son," I heard Death say;
    "I did not will a grave
Should end thy pilgrimage to-day,
    But I, too, am a slave!"

V

We smiled upon each other then,
    And life to me had less
Of that fell look it wore ere when
    They owned their passiveness.

"The Subalterns" exploits the ability of lyric poetry to take any side of a question. The speaker can be anyone: here the "I" has the last word, but not before the sky, North, Sickness, and Death have each had their say. These entities are answering questions we readers are forced to supply—not a difficult task, for surely most of the questions contain the word "why." Instead of questions we are given the answers—answers that, however unsatisfactory, are less hackneyed than the questions would be.

It is refreshing and intriguing that "The Subalterns," like moments in the *Iliad*, approaches suffering from the inhuman viewpoint of its agents rather than its victims—except that those agents turn out to be victims too, equally caught in a cosmic chain of command. The poem can be read as fatalistic, bitterly ironic, or (as Davie points out) harshly humorous. In the light of the kingdom of illness, it struck me as each of these things, but above all, as true. After all, if we were to question illness, what could it say—and indeed, what would we say? Our attempts to explain why people get sick run the risk either of assuming affectless scientific jargon or, even worse, of buying into a blame-the-victim approach that holds people accountable for what are hideously called lifestyle choices. At least Hardy's subalterns do not blame the "wight" for being cold, or sick, or dying.

I happened upon "The Subalterns" when I was visiting a friend for two snatched days in April. In May, George's health took a turn; to the suppurating skin rashes were added fever and chills and exhaustion. An X-ray revealed fluid on a lung. So it was off to see yet another doctor, a pulmonary specialist at Columbia-Presbyterian. We took a taxi straight from one doctor's office in midtown to the lung man uptown.

It was one of the rare sparkling days in the mostly cool and gray month of May that year. Early in the afternoon, Riverside Drive was almost empty of cars, the streets of people, as if everyone else had something better, something real, to do. Still, the rich green tapestry of Riverside Park on our left was busy with strollers and nannies. The sandboxes in the playgrounds were full of toddlers, and joggers moved past. Everyone was enjoying the precious sunshine. A familiar poem suddenly floated into my head: "Because I could not stop for Death—/He kindly stopped for me."

Emily Dickinson's poem "Because I Could Not Stop for Death" is one that I'd known as long as I could remember.

> Because I could not stop for Death—
> He kindly stopped for me—
> The Carriage held but just Ourselves—
> And Immortality.
>
> We slowly drove—He knew no haste
> And I had put away
> My labor and my leisure too,
> For His Civility—
>
> We passed the School, where Children strove
> At Recess—in the Ring—

We passed the Fields of Gazing Grain—
We passed the Setting Sun—

Or rather—He passed Us—
The Dews drew quivering and chill—
For only Gossamer, my Gown—
My Tippet—only Tulle—

We paused before a House that seemed
A Swelling of the Ground—
The Roof was scarcely visible—
The Cornice—in the Ground—

Since then—'tis Centuries—and yet
Feels shorter than the Day
I first surmised the Horses' Heads
Were toward Eternity—

Because death figures so vividly here, could indeed be said to be the poem's protagonist, it's no stretch to think of this famous poem as being "about" death or immortality. But Emily Dickinson's sibylline poems are notoriously hard to tuck into pigeonholes of meaning. It's not my purpose here, even if it were possible, to wring every drop of signification out of these twenty-four short lines. Instead, I will put on blinders and take a very partial look.

Thinking about the ride the poem takes us on, I find myself especially struck, this time around, by the repetition of the verb "passed." Everything the pair in the carriage presumably see as they "slowly" drive is referred to not as something seen but as something passed. So does the world stand still while the lady and Death drive by? Yes and no. "We passed" the school, the fields—and then, unexpectedly, "We passed the Setting Sun— / Or rather—He passed Us—." What a rich little reversal! These lines suggest the slight confusion as to whether, when we think we see the sun setting, it's actually "us," the earth, who are moving. But more to the point, there is also a human angle in the poem's hesitation as to who is doing the passing. Again, living in the kingdom of illness helped me read freshly.

Do we look out at the world as we pass by? Or is it the world that passes while we stand still? Although we normally experience only one of these possibilities at a time, both could be said to be plausible. One effect of illness is to make us live on that double track: double, but not parallel. On one track there is the world of seasons, weekends, holidays, semesters; of vacations, newspaper headlines, trips to be taken, plans to be made. On the other track, there is the place of illness. The ill person and his or her companion, moving on their own urgent trajectory, may strongly feel that theirs is the really valid and compelling journey, in comparison to which the rest of life, as they pass it by, is a Potemkin village. Equally, it may sometimes feel as if they are standing still, paralyzed, getting nowhere, while everything and everyone else moves on. Illness is like old age in the way it relentlessly marginalizes its sufferers, transforming them from participants into spectators.

The double track, the confusing spatial uncertainty as to where the action is, spills over in Dickinson's poem into the contradictory perception of time in the final stanza: "Since then—'tis Centuries—and yet / Feels shorter than the Day / I first surmised the Horses' Heads / Were toward Eternity—." Without the familiar routine that fills one's days in the outside world, the passage of time turns out to be as tricky as the knowledge of who is and isn't in motion.

In its sudden access of power, the unassuming verb "pass" seems as loaded in this poem as the equally workaday verb "turn" in "Home Burial." To pass, to turn—these everyday actions, verbs which can be found in sports parlance or a driver's manual, are remarkably rich in the human significance of the body language they suggest. To pass by, to turn away—such moves suggest that somebody is left behind, but even in so doing they assume an encounter of sorts. Because of the glass walls of the kingdom of illness, encounters are problematic—sparse, awkward, strange. Those on the outside make "the best of their way back to life," as the wife in "Home Burial" phrases it. Those on the inside may in any case be too busy to hear what (if anything) others say to them. They pass by the workaday world with its fields and its schoolchildren, and they may seem to outsiders as unfriendly as outsiders may seem to them.

Poems, though, never turn away. We can pass them by, we can turn the page; they wait patiently. Their feelings are not hurt. Their information effortlessly crosses the barricade between sickness and health.

2

"Home Burial" is clearly about bereavement; "The Subalterns" is about the questions we pose when things go wrong; "Because I Could Not Stop" is about (among other things) the way the journey to or with death cuts us off from the ongoing rhythms of life. I am oversimplifying here, but I'm not distorting, not wrenching these poems loose from their contexts. But it may be that some of the other things I was reading or remembering in the spring of 2005 only seemed relevant because I was spinning or tweaking or skewing them a little. I couldn't help it. "Memory and experience press themselves into each reading," as Allegra Goodman puts it, and I was experiencing the uncanniness of marriage to someone with whom it was almost impossible to carry on a conversation. The silence and loneliness, the anger and sadness, the confusion and sense of entrapment: from unexpected pages, all these feelings in turn looked back at me.

So far as I know, none of the following passages was written with dementia in mind. The sole possible exception is an Emily Dickinson poem which, as the critic Rick Barot points out, "may be talking about sin . . . [or] may be talking about dementia." This poem could also be about the decay of any relationship. Whatever her precise topic, Dickinson captures the theme of the extreme insidiousness of the loss.

> Crumbling is not an instant's Act
> A fundamental pause
> Dilapidation's processes
> Are organized Decays.
>
> 'Tis first a Cobweb on the Soul
> A Cuticle of Dust
> A Borer in the Axis
> An Elemental Rust—
>
> Ruin is formal—Devil's work
> Consecutive and slow—
> Fail in an instant, no man did
> Slipping—is Crash's law.

Examples were everywhere. Here, in an essay about rereading Hans Christian Andersen's "The Snow Queen," Barbara Sjoholm offers a cameo of the loyal and determined Gerda's quest to rescue Kai that reads to me like an allegory of the challenges faced by the spouse of a person with dementia—an allegory, however, that has a happy ending.

> Never wavering in her belief that [Kai] is alive, she [Gerda] sails, walks, rides in a carriage, and is carried by a reindeer to the Snow Queen's palace, where Kai has been doing little but racking his brain over broken pieces of ice, trying to spell a forgotten word.

And here is Lydia Davis, an expert and eloquent writer about the hazards of communication, in her book *Varieties of Disturbance,* on what we might assume is a married couple who aren't getting along.

> Soon almost every subject they might want to talk about is associated with yet another unpleasant scene and becomes a subject they can't talk about, so that as time goes by there is

less and less they can safely talk about, and eventually little else but the news and what they're reading, though not all of what they're reading.

Stir in the dementia factor, which means that one of the parties will be doing very little reading anyway, and Davis's passage is an excellent description of the kind of marital strain I experienced myself and heard plenty about from others.

Philip Larkin was a specialist in loneliness, including the kind of loneliness you experience when you're not alone, which may be the most acute loneliness of all. I found myself reading Larkin's "Talking in Bed" with fresh attention.

> Talking in bed ought to be easiest,
> Lying together there goes back so far,
> An emblem of two people being honest.
>
> Yet more and more time passes silently.
> Outside, the wind's incomplete unrest
> Builds and disperses clouds about the sky,
>
> And dark towns heap up on the horizon.
> None of this cares for us. Nothing shows why
> At this unique distance from isolation
>
> It becomes still more difficult to find
> Words at once true and kind
> Or not untrue and not unkind.

Philip Larkin presumably didn't write that poem for the spouses or bedmates of victims of neurodegenerative diseases. Nevertheless, "Talking in Bed" is every bit as much a resource as the neurologist, the social worker, or the support group. The poem's final tercet captures a truth about trying to talk to someone with dementia that I have rarely seen acknowledged, let alone so crisply and authoritatively put.

"At this unique distance from isolation" is the place where, when your spouse has dementia, you live. With luck, it can also be the place where poetry speaks—speaks all the more audibly, perhaps, in the thickening silence. The poetry may very well not be kind, but it may be true. And in that truth may inhere the only kindness available.

CHAPTER 8

Similes

Crises burn themselves into our memories, but as soon as the days take on something like a familiar rhythm, one ceases to pay much attention. In the fall of 2005, I went back to teaching, so outside the house my days were much less lonely. George's skin problems were better, finally—he had been hospitalized in June with a long-undiagnosed staph infection that quickly responded to intravenous medication. Now that he was no longer teaching, how did he spend his days? Lots of cigarette walks in the park, sports on TV, listening to CDs, mostly Bach and Schütz. Every morning he bought the newspaper, though he didn't really read it, and sometimes he would buy a bottle of wine (always at a nearby store, Gotham Wines & Liquors at Ninety-fourth Street and Broadway) or some St. André cheese (always the same kind of cheese, and always at Gourmet Garage at Ninety-sixth and Broadway). Maybe he tried to compose a little. Occasionally I'd gather my courage to ask, "Aren't you bored?" and he would say, "I have inner resources."

So was this time a period of what psychologists call the new normal? Yes and no. Remember the kingdom of illness; remember the double track. George and I were in a new world that looked quite a lot like the old world, especially because we'd been slipping into it slowly for so long. But it was *not* the old world, not for him, and not for me when I was with him. George didn't converse with anyone. He didn't use the telephone or the Internet. His occasional lunches with old friends were events I carefully scheduled, as if I were making playdates for a small child. They were uphill work for George's lunch companions, and soon they stopped. It wasn't clear how much he understood about his own condition—and that was only one of many things in our lives that weren't clear.

As usual, I wanted more clarity than the situation afforded, and the relatively uneventful academic year 2005–06 was a chance to do some thinking about our situation. The illness was beginning to look familiar, but what should we expect? Where were we going and how fast would we get there? How to think, how to talk about an experience that defied precision? That these questions were unanswerable didn't mean I wasn't grasping for answers. As always, literature provided what I needed. Poems like Frost's "Home Burial" or Hardy's "The Subalterns" cast light on human extremity, but now I was trying to puzzle out a process. Similes unexpectedly helped me think about what was going on with George and me.

Early in 2006, I had a chance to hear a good deal of the *Iliad* read aloud at a marathon event (in which I participated) hosted by a group called the Readers of Homer. Book Three of the epic opens with a spectacular series of similes that follow one upon another in close succession. The Trojan army marches out as noisily as cranes; the dust stirred up by the feet of the silent Greek army resembles mist on the mountains; Menelaus strides out to confront Paris as fiercely as a lion devours the carcass of a stag or wild goat; and Paris, seeing Menelaus, jumps backward like a man who has just been frightened by a snake.

> After the captains had marshaled their ranks
> those Trojans marched out clamorous as birds,
> like cranes that clamor under the heavens
> when they flee from winter's torrential rains
> and, crying wildly, fly toward Oceanus,
> bringing death and fate for the Pygmy men
> and foully battle them at early dawn—

but the Achaeans marched out silently,
planning how to help their fellow warriors.
As the South Wind covers mountains in mist,
a curse for shepherds, camouflage for thieves,
and men see only a stone's throw ahead,
so the clouds of dust whirled up from their feet
when they hurried over the Trojan plain.
After those armies came near each other,
prince Paris pranced out before his people,
on his back a leopardskin and a bow
and his sword. Brandishing two bronze-tipped spears,
he challenged any Achaean leader
to meet him man-to-man in awful war.
When Atreus' son Menelaus spied him
striding out mightily before them all
he was glad as a hungry lion who finds
a great carcass of some stag or wild goat
and greedily enjoys a hearty meal
though hunters surround him with their quick hounds—
so Menelaus was glad to see Paris
because he expected revenge at last
and leaped from his chariot in full armor.
But when godlike Paris saw Menelaus
appearing among the foremost, his heart
sank, and he slunk back among his comrades.
As a man retreats when he sees a snake
in a mountain valley and starts to shake,
then hurries away, his cheeks deadly pale:
thus that godlike Alexander shrank back
among his men, for fear of Atreus' son.

(translated by Michael Reck)

These similes came as a distinct relief to us hearers, supplying a change of texture and pace, a break in the action. The fierce, headlong start of the epic—the angry exchanges, Achilles' thwarted impulse to attack Agamemnon, his subsequent plea to his goddess mother for help—these events in Book One don't afford the reader or listener a moment's respite, and Book Two isn't much more tranquil until the Catalogue of Ships interrupts the action. The power of the opening of Book Three, then, is all the more striking because of both the unremitting pace of what has come before and the newness, early in the epic's unfolding, of the effect similes create. The narrative voice—the voice of the epic—is speaking, and it is an easier voice to listen to than the fraught rage of Homer's larger-than-life heroes.

Similes aren't merely a decorative literary device; they're functional. They help us to see freshly, to make new connections. They offer a change of perspective, and they provide a kind of relief on the battlefield of life as well as on the battlefield of Homeric epic. Wallace Stevens wrote that the imagination, by pressing back against the pressure of reality, helps us to live our lives. When I try to think of a specific function or manifestation of the imagination that is helpful, similes are what occur to me.

Stevens's "Notes Toward a Supreme Fiction," an extended poetic meditation on the workings of the imagination, offers up the radiant line, "Life's nonsense pierces us with strange relation." As much good poetry has always done, this line has recently snapped into focus for me in a way the poet certainly didn't intend. (Perhaps this elasticity is a defining characteristic of poetry that retains its vitality.) I have come to think of similes as able to capture that relation in all its strangeness. It might also turn out that similes manage to meet all three of the requirements that "Notes" asks of Supreme Fiction: "it must be abstract," "it must change," and "it must give pleasure." For as George ever so slowly sinks further into apathy, passivity, and silence, I find myself in urgent daily need of just these three commodities. As a poet, a teacher, and above all a human being, I need these gifts of the imagination if I am going to cope. They are not sufficient, but they are damned well necessary.

Even the most sympathetic doctors write no prescriptions for the imagination, so I must give these gifts to myself. Fortunately, as Homer evidently knew, similes lie around everywhere, waiting to be discovered. By 2006, when the uncanniness of living with a man who couldn't carry on a conversation but could scamper around a tennis court had crept into every nook and cranny of my days and infiltrated my dreams, certain similes came to my aid, opening windows to let in light and air. They helped to lift me a little way above the battlefield of living alongside someone with dementia—a battlefield not of epic heroism but of remorseless, grinding boredom, of endless petty tasks and bureaucratic challenges, of pervasive loneliness. Similes gave and still give me a space from which to scan the terrain and see what my life—our lives—actually look like.

Similes can and do pop into my head like textbook examples of comparisons with "like or as," but they can also be more dynamic than this formula might suggest. When we were first given something like a diagnosis in early 2005, George asked if he would get better. The neurologist replied that his condition was "permanent and progressive."

This tidy alliterative package, like many simple formulations, wasn't easy to think about. The first half of it suggested stasis, the second motion. Pondering George's condition meant somehow reconciling the two, and soon I started envisioning a one-way road on which it was possible to drive at various speeds, or even to stop for a while. There might be an occasional detour, some of the scenery might even be quite pretty, but there was no turning around and going back.

During 2005 and 2006, we'd been dawdling along this one-way thoroughfare. As I conceived of it, the road was lonely; we might be the only people traveling in our—wait, was it a car? To the idea of a road I now added a vivid picture of a vehicle—not a car but, illogically enough, a train, a very slow local train making every possible stop along the way. Having started its long journey at this poky pace, the train seemed likely to continue traveling pretty much that way, though one couldn't rule out sudden and unpredictable bursts of speed.

Above the road, above the train tracks, the sky was cloudy. Every now and then the sun would break through; sometimes the whole sky would clear. But sooner or later, and usually sooner, the sun would disappear again. The curious thing was that whenever the sun was out, the whole day seemed likely to go on being sunny, but when it hid behind a cloud, the mood of the day instantly, and apparently permanently, changed. "Why did'st thou promise such a beauteous day / And make me travel forth without my cloak, / To let base clouds o'ertake me on my way, / Hiding thy bravery in their rotten smoke?" Shakespeare asks the sun reproachfully in Sonnet 34. I knew the feeling.

The one-way road, the slow train, the uncertain sky: all these helped me, if not to understand what was going on, then to understand how little I could do about it and, with this understanding, to manage the ups and downs, the fitful bursts of sunshine succeeded by more clouds.

There were fewer sunny spots by late in 2006, but there were also fewer bursts of George's anger—bursts for which it occurred to me I functioned like a surge protector. Surge protector, shield, buffer, padding, interpreter—none of these similes was quite right, but all were useful to the degree that they helped me to get my mind around my almost inconceivable and certainly indescribable new role by seeing it with some semblance of Homeric objectivity—a quality recognized by critics from Longinus to Matthew Arnold as noble and sublime, which also turns out to be quotidian, demotic, and handy.

As George's anger ebbed, the reproachful notes left for me on the dining room table became a thing of the past. They might reappear, but given the one-way nature of the journey, I doubted that they would. Unless he was hungry or suddenly roused from sleep, George now did not say anything biting or reproachful, to me or anyone else. He said hardly anything at all. When he did speak, it was almost always to answer a question. I kept intending, and then somehow failing, to test this observation by refraining from putting my customary questions to him. Obviously, I didn't really want to know how few words he uttered of his own accord in the course of a day.

Typical questions I asked George included: Are you ready for lunch now? What's it like out? How are the Braves doing? Are you okay? This last one felt like a clumsy approximation of inquiring of someone with a severe physical disability if he's comfortable. Since below the neck George was fine, and above the neck he was not and would not be, it was the wrong question—but there were no right questions. Similes, language at play in the absence of dialogue, filled in some of the gap.

A striking feature of George's vanishingly sparse speech was that he virtually never used the pronoun "I," as in "I'm tired," "I'm hungry," "I want . . ." When my sister, Beth, was visiting, she sat down at the dining room table one day for a mid-morning snack of crackers and cheese. George silently drifted in from the living room and sat down opposite her at the table, eyeing her plate (as she said later) "like a cow coming up to the fence." I think the poet of the *Iliad* would have appreciated this precise little trope, which was mildly comical, mildly pathetic, and wholly apt. Beth's other contribution to my useful stock of George-related similes was also perfectly right, but out of Disney rather than Homer. I commented on George's rapid daily walks. "Yes," she said, "just think of him as a tall hamster." This image took on a surreal life of its own when at least one person spontaneously revised it into "giant hamster." But everyone who heard it laughed: it was funny, and right, and helpful. In the world of dementia, a laugh, like a simile, is something they don't write prescriptions for.

If the cow at the fence and the tall hamster were serviceable similes, here's an example of one I found to be the opposite of helpful. Like some illnesses, this simile is iatrogenic; its source is a physician. It was offered by the first neurologist we consulted. She asked me how I was doing; my answer must have been less than ebullient.

"You know how it is when you move from one house to another?" she said. "In the new house, you can live in a state of transition for a long time, with piles of boxes all over the place. Or you can really move in and make yourself at home. I don't think you've completely moved in yet."

Of course I understood what the doctor was getting at. One does indeed habituate to surprising things. (I was going to say "to almost anything.") In some ways, yes, it was easier for me to live with George in 2006 than it had been in 2004 or 2005, and so perhaps I had made some progress toward settling into the new house offered in the neurologist's simile. But what kind of house was it, and to what kind of new life was I getting accustomed? The neurologist did not ask these questions, which it is the business of similes not only to raise but to answer.

Living alongside a husband with dementia is, in my experience, exhausting and boring, lonely and frustrating. (And I have a good deal of help taking care of George; without help it would be completely demoralizing and destructive.) If I hadn't unpacked all those boxes and moved right in, was I to blame? The more I thought about it, the more I resisted the neurologist's simile, which proved to be prophetic of her ability to make me feel inadequate and guilty at every turn. A few months later, I found another neurologist, one who didn't make me feel like a failure.

If living with a spouse suffering from dementia is to be compared to living in a house, let's at least find the right kind of house for the comparison. You're married to someone; you have presumably made a commitment, and you trustingly assume a relation of lasting reciprocity with the person you have chosen to spend the rest of your life with. But slowly and insidiously your partner changes from the person you married into someone else, someone who, while he still dwells alongside you, no longer cares about your well-being, who may in fact actively wish you ill. The structure you inhabit with this person is no longer a shared household, a cozy refuge. It now resembles a prison that mocks you with the fact that you long ago entered it voluntarily—and a prison, furthermore, where you have become responsible for the daily care of a warden who has mysteriously changed into a ward.

The notion of marriage as a trap or jail has been beautifully and terrifyingly developed by both Edith Wharton in her story "The Reckoning" and Henry James in *The Portrait of a Lady.* Both convey the tenor of the wife's thoughts in tropes that equate marriage with house and house with prison.

Wharton:

> Her husband's personality seemed to be closing gradually in on her, obscuring the sky and cutting off the air, till she felt herself shut up among the decaying bodies of her starved hopes. A sense of having been decoyed by some world-old conspiracy into this bondage of body and soul filled her with despair. If marriage was the slow life-long acquittal of a debt contracted in ignorance, then marriage was a crime against human nature.

And James, in a passage where Isabel Archer broods about her marriage to Gilbert Osmond:

> She could live it over again, the incredulous terror with which she had taken the measure of her dwelling. Between those four walls she had lived ever since; they were to surround her for the rest of her life. It was the house of darkness, the house of dumbness, the house of suffocation . . . Of course it had not been physical suffering; for physical suffering there might have been a remedy.

Are these passages too grim? Possibly; but the neurologist's chirpy evocation of living with dementia as moving into a new house and getting used to it is assuredly not grim enough. Living with someone with dementia doesn't always feel like being imprisoned, but that is *one* of the things it certainly does feel like. "For physical suffering there might have been a remedy"—how poignantly true this is, for my husband as much as, or more than, for me. I've often caught myself wishing he had a visible disability, so that other people and I, myself, would be reminded of his impairment and so make allowances better. I am not literally imprisoned—I am free to get up and go. But getting up and going are easier said than done.

So this, I want to shout, is what it feels like. There's the one-way road and the changeable sky; the cow at the fence and the tall hamster; and the prison house called marriage. And I remember now that the walled garden I used to envision as surrounding my husband before we were married, when I'd first fallen in love with him, was enticing, in part, precisely because it was so forbidding. Be careful what you wish for: Here I am, immured alongside him.

Yet not wholly immured. The truth—for which there is no prescription any more than there is for laughter—does help. How? It's hard to say. Similes, the branch of truth I've been exploring, do not reassure. They connect; they clarify. And a modicum of clarity is as precious in the foggy world of dementia as Galadriel's vial in *The Lord of the Rings*, shedding a beam of light in our own private Shelob's lair—a realm where, as the latest neurologist recently summed up, "a firm diagnosis remains elusive." It feels appropriate that George's illness cannot be named with precision. "Your husband," said another one of the doctors, "didn't walk out of a textbook." But no one can stop me from saying what I think it resembles, and so conveying what it feels like, and so making some slight progress in understanding it.

CHAPTER 9

Ambiguous Loss

Meanwhile, similes or no similes, the silence at home went grindingly on. The silence could be somber or glowering, reproachful or opaque, or even sometimes mildly contented. Although I knew perfectly well that silence was George's default mode, it was hard to construe it as neutral. At night, when I wasn't writing or doing schoolwork, I would talk on the phone to my sister or a friend after George was asleep. Then I'd go to bed, where I usually slept soundly, cocooned by the depth of his sleep, borrowing a fold of the unconsciousness that swaddled him. I always went to bed long after George did and tried to get up long before he did, though in this latter effort I was rarely successful. He'd go around the corner to the newsstand at Broadway and 101st Street to buy the *Times*, and when he returned he'd sit at the table, waiting to be served breakfast and begin another empty day.

Needless to say, any conversation had to be initiated by me. A woman in one of my support groups whose husband has had Parkinson's for thirty years describes her attempts to keep up some chitchat at mealtimes as a song and dance. She's exactly right: such an effort is a performance. My own take on the unilateral nature of this "exchange" is expressed in my poem "Monodrama," which, like many of the poems I was beginning to write, infuses a literary genre with my personal dilemma.

In the fall of 2006, I was teaching a course in Victorian poetry—a rare opportunity, given that it isn't really my field (I was filling in for a colleague on sabbatical leave). Dipping into some of what scholars had recently written about Victorian poetry, I was struck by critical emphasis on the various versions of dramatic monologue, for which Victorian poets had a great affinity.

Monodrama

Before the phrase "dramatic monologue"
was coined, Victorian poets
seem to have had recourse to other terms,
among them many starting with "dramatic":
as in dramatic lyrics or romances,
dramatic idylls, studies, or dramatis
personae. But my favorite of all
these labels is the shortest: monodrama.
I like the single word's simplicity,
the asymmetrically lurching gait,
the austere paradox as of one hand clapping:
a unilateral dialogue. I don't
exactly like but certainly acknowledge
how close to home this hits. Has not my life
felt for years now like a monodrama?
Everyone feels this, maybe, as they age.
Adolescents for that matter feel it.
And surely every woman. Every wife.
Everyone married to a person walled
into silence: mine the drama, his
the mono, as he's sealed in, brick by brick.

Those bricks at the conclusion remind me of—maybe they derive from—Poe's story "The Cask of Amontillado." I suspect that the notion of being walled in isn't an uncommon way of visualizing the slowly accruing effects of dementia. In her memoir *The Story of My Father*, Sue Miller refers to her father's Alzheimer's having "closed over" his ability to read.

Walled in. At a birthday celebration for the great Alexandrian poet C. P. Cavafy one recent spring (he was born in 1863, and his work is going strong), when I heard his very familiar "Walls" read aloud, the poem said something new.

> With no consideration, no pity, no shame,
> they have built walls around me, thick and high.
> And now I sit here feeling hopeless.
> I can't think of anything else: this fate gnaws my mind—
> because I had so much to do outside.
> When they were building the walls, how could I not have
>   noticed!
> But I never heard the builders, not a sound.
> Imperceptibly they have closed me off from the outside world.
>
> *(translated by Edmund Keeley)*

These walls beg for a figurative reading. What they evoke or symbolize is a rich variety of moods and situations—isolation, depression, and old age are only three of the more obvious. This time, as I listened to the poem, it was immediately clear to me that "Walls" was about the stealthy progress of the kind of incurable condition George was grappling with— a disease often not even noticeable until it's well established.

Cavafy is more interested in the sufferer's reaction than in the stealthy progress itself, and he has it right—at least for this companion of the sufferer. One does feel hopeless, unable to think of anything else. This fate most certainly does gnaw one's mind. One wonders over and over, "How could I not have noticed!" And finally, one is indeed closed off from the outside world, sealed into a place of steadily encroaching silence.

Circling this central silence, I seem to have approached it like a math problem. Wasn't there something quantitative about the exchange, the give and take of ordinary dialogue? But I was never good at math, and this was a devilish arithmetic: nothing seemed to add up. Where a fresh start might have been needed, I found myself unable to come up with anything. Until habituation had begun its gradual task of rendering the silence inaudible, the emptiness invisible, this silence and emptiness weren't neutral, they were aggressive.

Poetry let me try to pose the problem afresh, balance the equation. The following three short poems all have a speciously quantitative quality, as if I were keeping accounts, but what they try to quantify is nullity.

Minus

Economy of loss: the sly
subtraction whereby
I give when I have nothing left to give

and nothing is acknowledged. When there might
be something I can offer, I refuse.
The brassy taste of emptiness persists.

"The Beam" injects into this pseudo-mathematical mix the image of my own frustrated seeking as a searchlight sweeping the darkness.

The Beam

What I have to give you you don't want
or cannot any longer recognize.
What you still seem to want or need I give
grudgingly, then less and less, and not.

What I need you no longer can give me,
and both of us are angry. So I turn
away and have for years,
though rooted to the spot,

been turning like a beam,
a searchlight hopefully

or doggedly from sheer
habit raking the gloom.

In this world of failed exchanges, there's one commodity of which there is no lack. Perhaps it's a remainder or a lowest common denominator. My poem about this commodity, though, edges away from treating the problem as one of mathematics.

Loneliness

Love costs anxiety, joy has a price:
the fragile edge and smoky smell of limits.
    Loneliness
lacks any such suggestion of an end.
    It is forever,
and plentiful beyond imagining.
    Whatever realm it comes from
boasts a supply not only infinite
but constantly increasing. This is one
resource we need not fear will be depleted.
Nor do we need to doubt that anyone
who once has tasted loneliness will ever
    forget its special savor.

Does everyone's loneliness share a certain savor, or is each person's loneliness peculiar to them? The poem leaves room for both possibilities. Part of the particular savor of my own loneliness had to do with the fact that George was physically present—in fact was nearly always at home—but in other ways was increasingly absent. In her book *Ambiguous Loss*, Pauline Boss writes helpfully about the challenges dementia poses to mourners who must cope with physical presence and psychological absence, as well as the reverse challenges—bodily absence, psychological presence—that arise, for example, when a loved one is serving in the military overseas, perhaps missing in action. In both cases, the process of grieving, never clear and simple, is even more confusing; there's no death to mourn.

Part of the process of mourning someone we've lost involves finding a way to recover that person, to get him back, if only in intermittent flashes. But when the loss is ambiguous, so is the getting-back part. It was hard for me to find an access to the vanished George, the George I had lost, in part because the new and altered George was so constantly before my eyes. Not surprisingly, then, some of the moments when I felt his old, undiminished presence most strongly occurred when I was physically distant from him and so could envision or imagine him—could assess the entire situation—from a fresh perspective. So long as he was still living at home, these moments were few.

For example, at a fall 2006 conference in Cambridge, Massachusetts, a place I hadn't visited in years, the heavy cover on the hotel bed reminded me that I missed George's physical presence in the bed next to me. And this sense of loss, this unusual pang of wanting him to be in the same space I found myself in, unexpectedly brought back his and my visits many years before to his mother, who lived in Wellesley. These visits took place in 1977 and 1978, before a disabling stroke early in 1979 changed this exuberant and independent woman to a spectral shadow of herself, and in the process changed her family's relation to her to one of ambiguous loss—a state of affairs that would drag on from 1979 to her death in 2001.

Faux Fur

Something about the heavy
throw on the hotel bed,
the coverlet, dark mink,
striped satin on the back;

the leopard print of robe
and carpet (wall to wall)
made me miss you. Made
me feel the weight of your

constricted life; somehow
allowed me to distinguish
the past once it was far enough away.
Twenty-five years ago,

closer to thirty, we
used to come to Boston,
staying with your mother
in Wellesley. She was healthy.

You and I were young,
or relatively young,
and full of hope. I try
now to remember: did

it feel in those days as
if the future stretched
lightly out ahead?
Lightness gives way to weight:

grey mist over the river,
nap under dark brown fur.
W. H. Auden
preferred to sleep well anchored:

he'd spread his overcoat
over the blankets, then
for good measure maybe
a volume of the *O*.

E. D.; to top it off
perhaps a big framed picture
he'd taken from the wall.
Frame, glass were reassuring:

he would insert himself
underneath these strata
and go straight to sleep.
Weight, fur—I needed these

to feel how I had lost you,
lost what you used to be,
pressing on my prone body,
and so to get you back.

"Faux Fur" refers in passing to George's mother and moves right on, but it's worth pausing to note that in her twenty-two years of disability, Connie both was and wasn't there for George and his brother and sister.

The concept of ambiguous loss is also easy to apply to figures in literature. Although Pauline Boss doesn't mention her, Penelope in the *Odyssey* is surely the archetype of a woman poised, or paralyzed, between alternatives. Odysseus has been gone for twenty years; he left for Troy when their son was a baby, the war went on for ten years, and for the past ten he has been, perhaps, traveling home to Ithaca. Penelope has raised their child and has waited. Should she make up her mind that her husband is dead, mourn for him, move on, remarry? The shroud she weaves and unweaves is a fitting emblem of the unfinished and unfinishable work of mourning when we don't know whether to mourn or not—when perhaps we hardly know what to mourn. Penelope uses the unfinished condition of the shroud (a condition she herself creates by unweaving each night what she has woven the day before) as a ploy to fend off the pressing attentions of her suitors. It's easy to forget that the shroud is said to be intended for her father-in-law, Laertes, who is old but very much alive; it feels equally like the grave-cloth for the absent Odysseus, or even for their marriage.

At least as memorable as the happy ending of the *Odyssey*, in which Odysseus and Penelope are reunited, are both the twenty years of their separation and their flickering on-and-off exchange leading up to the deferred reunion. Odysseus is of course in disguise throughout this portion of the narrative, but Penelope is playing her cards close to her chest, too: Is she wife or widow, naive or sly, calculating or lost? All in turn? All at once? How could I fail to see that all these facets of Penelope were parts of my story, too?

I first read the *Odyssey* in Robert Fitzgerald's translation when I was about twelve. The story and the poetry enchanted me. In college, I read the first few books of it in Greek with my wonderful professor Gregory Nagy. I found that I would choke up if asked to talk about Telemachus in class; my father had died that August, shortly before the start of my sophomore year, and I saw his absence everywhere. Later still, when I was the mother of a roving teenaged son, I understood perfectly Penelope's anxiety over Telemachus's voyage. And now, neither wife nor widow, suspended in an open-ended period that was and was not waiting, enmeshed in the web of ambiguous loss, I understand Penelope again, newly, better.

The Flickering Reunion

The waiting, and the pacing, and the weaving.

I have found a figure for my loneliness, and this figure,
or the story in which the figure is embedded and embodied,
has the effect of bringing pity back,
as stories can, while books
with titles like *Ambiguous Loss* cannot.
Powerfully the story activates
pity for self and pity for the other
through the medium of the Yes and No
where No trumps Yes, then waveringly recedes.

In this flickering reunion,
I live with No but Yes lurks somewhere near,

Yes in fact is never wholly gone,
is ineradicable so long as we live together,
I and this semi-stranger in his acrid rags
whose history is so intertwined with mine
he has never really left, he cannot leave;
yet he is also long and gradually gone.

You reach a point, or we do, or she does,
where pronouns cease to matter:
the woman who stands still, then turns and paces
and goes upstairs again and naps and weeps
is scolded by her only son.
Fearing for him, she scolds him in return.

The waiting, and the pacing, and the weaving.
She's not a widow, but she sleeps alone.

CHAPTER 10

Who He Was

If the reunion between Odysseus and Penelope flickers in and out of focus, if loss is ambiguous, it's because there is something left. In 2005, 2006, and 2007, George was physically unchanged: tall, lithe, graceful, blue-eyed, with brown hair untinged by gray. When his skin troubles cleared up, his skin went back to being soft and fine. There was never an ounce of fat on his body; all his joints were flexible. He always looked and moved like a much younger man than he was.

How did he feel? What was he thinking? It's impossible to say for sure. As the dementia deepened, two things happened: it became more difficult for him to put his thoughts and feelings into words; and he had less and less insight into what was happening to him. "No insight and no empathy," wrote neurologist number two, a Philadelphia specialist, in a report in 2007. But in 2005 and 2006, perhaps some insight and empathy remained. Perhaps some still remain.

The various neuropsychological and other tests George underwent late in 2004 and early in 2005 revealed a disease process fairly far advanced. His lonely struggle to marshal the right words, to remember what had to be done, to recall conversations, to keep appointments, to prepare classes, to write recommendations and program notes—all this had been going on since at least 2002. I figured this out later, talking to George's colleagues and coming upon a few heartbreaking drafts of a simple program note for "Venetian Swell," probably the last composition he completed.

> *Venetian Swell* (2003) could refer to the constant danger of floods in Venice. But while my piece refers frequently to the rhythms of the typical Barcarolle, I also had a image in mind. For a Venetian Swell is also a term to describe some rather decadent which use bellows (activated by the player's knees) to enable the player to produce cresendi and dimandi which are otherwise uncharistic of the instrument . . .

These few mistake-riddled sentences cost a good deal of effort: drafts, false starts, crossings-out. But he never asked for help, never said he was having difficulties.

What I remember now are a few stray things George did say about his condition after he stopped working at the end of 2004—isolated sentences, marooned in the surrounding silence, but all the more poignant therefore. These gnomic utterances are hard to date (early 2005, most of them); they became fewer as time went on.

He asked the first neurologist we consulted whether he would get better.

He said to me once, "I'm so sorry to visit this on you."

He said, when I had been away for a day or two and asked him what he'd been doing, "I've been doing a lot of crying."

He said to me once, speaking, I think, of his difficulties teaching, "I never knew how much I'd be able to remember," or "I never knew what I'd be able to do."

He said, "I think I'll be able to go on composing, because that comes out of my own head."

He said to me a few, a very few, times, but more than once, "I don't know what I'd do without you."

He said—this was the summer of 2006, I think, and we were sitting on the porch of the house in Vermont one evening after dinner—"I've been very lucky." I wanted him to say more, but I didn't want to put words in his mouth, so I just agreed.

The inner resources George sometimes referred to when I asked him if he wasn't bored—I know they were real, at least for a while. He may have been composing in his head, or listening to music in his head, or thinking about happy times in Rome. He continued playing the piano—short, familiar pieces, Bach or Chopin—after he stopped reading.

It was George who taught me to listen to music. Growing up in an unmusical home, totally untrained in music, I had enjoyed listening to my parents' classical LPs of Beethoven, Mozart, Haydn, and a few other things: my mother adored Prokofiev's Lieutenant Kijé Suite, and both my parents liked Gilbert and Sullivan. Either a high-school boyfriend introduced me to Corelli and Telemann and Purcell, or else I discovered them and English madrigals on my own. That was about the extent of my acquaintance with music. Soon after we met, George got me to sit down and listen to the music he loved: Schubert, Schumann, Chopin, Mahler, Wagner. "Sit down, be quiet," he'd say, kindly but firmly. We listened to a lot of Bach—not just the Brandenburg Concertos, which I already knew and loved, but the Passions. It was the *St. John Passion*, around Easter 1977, when we were still living on Claremont Avenue, that made him cry, or that brought to the surface tears that had been accumulating inside him. Music also made George laugh, and sometimes it still does— a laughter of joy but also of appreciation of wit, as at a punch line. He responded to, and wrote eloquently about, the wit in Haydn.

George's own music is witty, that much I know, but others are far better equipped than I am to talk about how and why. I have to say that much of the twentieth-century music we heard premiered—and we heard a lot of it in the early years— struck me as deadly serious, and often as ugly and dull. One of the many reasons I'm grateful George wrote his essays and they found a publisher is that his wit expresses itself so well in language. Let me quote from George's Columbia colleague

Joseph Dubiel, who contributed the afterword to George's *Collected Essays on Modern and Classical Music*:

> Anyone who has ever met George knows what a witty man he is, and something of George's wit seems to rub off on people's descriptions of him. A colleague once referred to George's "humane but unsentimental intelligence"; even when he hurts us, he makes us love it. Once in a department meeting, we were having a discussion of the system of grading to be used for students receiving academic credit for playing in the Columbia University Orchestra: Pass/Fail, as had been the case, or A-through-F, as some students wished. This is the sort of issue it is easy to make look silly, but it is important in the contexts to which it is important; which is not to say that the deliberations are sustainedly fascinating to those not directly involved. Bored, at a certain point, I indulged myself in the suggestion, "If they play quietly, give them a P; if they play loud, give them an F," and felt momentarily clever—until George's instantaneous response: "But now the concertmaster is asking for an A."

Even after George's verbal wit was crippled by dementia, he would still sometimes meet my eye as if to share the joke at a moment in a Haydn string quartet. When I told him that an article about President Obama and Chief Justice Roberts's verbal tug of war over the oath of office during the Presidential Inauguration was entitled "The Oaf of Office," George burst out laughing. Does his laughter still signify comprehension, though? Not always.

Sharing a joke with a wink; admonishing me to sit still and listen—when I think of such moments, I'm naturally reminded of what a wonderful father George was to our son, Jonathan. When I went into labor on the night of February 3, 1984, we'd been listening to Schubert's Ninth Symphony; George said afterward that Jon hadn't been able to resist coming into a world where there was such beautiful music. When we brought Jon home from the hospital, George softly played Schumann's "Kinderszenen" on the piano to greet him. In the early weeks and months, George would lay the infant on his knees while we listened to music; Jon would look up, calm and sparkling, into his father's face.

George effortlessly passed on to Jonathan his own love of and talent for chess and tennis, without ever huffing and puffing about it, without boasting or pressure or undue competitiveness on his own or his son's behalf. When Jon started piano lessons at the age of seven or so, George was always available to answer questions or to help, but he never pushed. Jon shared George's love for Chopin, and played—to my untrained ear at least—with some of his father's moody delicacy of touch. Jon's piano teacher said it made her laugh to see how, when entering a room or standing with his hands in his pockets or sitting down on a piano bench, Jon was a carbon copy of his father.

In the paternal role of disciplinarian, George had a gently creative approach: he invented the institution of the Talking Chair, which was an armchair to which father and son would repair to talk over whatever contretemps had transpired or whenever George declared a time-out. In New York, the Talking Chair was a big brown armchair; in Vermont, a moth-eaten recliner. In the summer of 1986, when we went to the Composers Conference on the Wellesley College campus, Jonathan, aged two and a half, asked his father, as we entered the dining room for the first time, where the Talking Chair was.

Jonathan remembers dancing with George to Handel's *Fireworks* and *Water Music*. We all enjoyed listening to *The Magic Flute* or Bruckner's Seventh Symphony as we drove up to Vermont. And I remember, when Jon was in elementary school, that George often used to walk him to school in the mornings. Standing at our living-room window, which faced north onto 101st Street, I could glimpse father and son marching up West End Avenue until they disappeared from view.

In our early years together, George was also gentle and fatherly with me. Sit down, sit still, listen: by precept and example, from the time we met at MacDowell Colony in 1976, he helped me to focus, to take myself seriously as a writer. I was having trouble sleeping. I remember George saying gravely, when I told him this, "You have to live in your body," by which I think he meant, "You have to take responsibility for your body." Later, he would tell me long, soothing, funny but boring bedtime stories (or rather, stories told in bed) about invented characters with names like Codger the Badger, Thatcher the Lodger, Anya the Author, and Wolfgang the Wolverine, to help me fall asleep at night. We laughed a lot, but I also relaxed. I helped embroider these tales, but it was George's deep-voiced, deliberately slowed-down delivery that would push me over the edge into sleep.

When I was first taking graduate seminars at Princeton, anxious and intimidated to find myself among younger students who all seemed thoroughly conversant with Derrida (even if they hadn't read much else), it was from George that I learned to say respectfully, "I disagree." It was also from George that I learned that the Arts and Leisure section of the Sunday *New York Times* was not the last word on cultural matters; that critics could be wrong-headed; that it was desirable to think for oneself in matters of aesthetics. I don't mean that I had no taste, no preferences; but I had little confidence in my own opinions and had done little thinking about principles. When I began teaching at Rutgers, George and I would discuss our ups and downs in the classroom, what worked, what didn't. Our conversation, which began as soon as we met, was wide-ranging and instructive and always pleasurable. One more memory from MacDowell, when we were first getting to know each other. (I can't believe how naive I was.) After his two years at the American Academy in Rome (1973–75), George had returned to the New England Conservatory for a year before coming to Columbia.

Rachel: You're a composer. So why is it that you teach music theory at the New England Conservatory?

George (poker-faced): In order to support my habit.

All these excellent memories seem as crucially formative and also as remote as memories of one's parents when one was young. I am reminded of what my first husband, Stavros—whose English, however imperfect, was expressive—said to me sadly when we were about to part ways: "I grew you up, and then you left me."

In many ways, even though I was twenty-seven when we met, George grew me up. His seriousness about his art, his independence of thought—these continue to be an example to me, an example I've so internalized that I don't consciously acknowledge it as often as I should. He is part of me. He helped me to become an adult; he helped to raise Jonathan, for the first twelve or so years of Jonathan's life. Then he began to leave us, and to leave himself.

CHAPTER 11

Old Leaves of
Abortive Memorials

Reading? Headlines in the *Times*; the occasional sports article, or at least the beginning of one; baseball box scores. Occasionally George used to take a book off the shelf, some old faithful: a mystery by Dick Francis, a novel by Kingsley Amis. Think of someone whose appetite has failed, reaching out for the foods they used to crave and hope they can somehow still enjoy.

Early on, I'd buy him books for Christmas—books about Italy or about Italian soccer. The last book he read and I think enjoyed was probably Joe McGinniss's *The Miracle of Castel di Sangro*—that and *Mussolini's Italy*. In 2007, he still bought the Italian soccer paper *La Gazzetta dello Sport*, "the pink paper," as we called it, on Sundays—and he usually seemed to know when it was Sunday. As long ago as the fall of 2004, when my willful blindness still shielded me from so much, I had noticed that he read the pink sports paper with far more attention than he did the Sunday *Times*, which he'd buy, glance at cursorily, and put down.

Writing? For a while, in the fall of 2006—this is an unpleasantly vivid memory—he would write me angry notes, which I'd find on the dining-room table in the evenings when I'd gone out and returned home after he was in bed. Those notes were bitter, accusatory, and by and large well written. Phrases like "my suspicions are confirmed" or "you too will realize that you are mortal" are carved into my memory.

That first neurologist we consulted told me that she found the notes (which I perhaps foolishly showed to her) touching. And so they were, in a way: they had their own poignant, indignant, wrecked eloquence. Perhaps it signaled a limitation on my part that I found them disturbing, even infuriating, no matter how much they told me about George's mental state. Perhaps, too, I should have taken care to archive them as I have some of George's other late writings, instead of throwing them away. But then neurologist number one made me feel like a failure no matter what I did. In any case, the notes soon stopped. By early 2009, George couldn't write at all any more—at most a scrawled signature with a barely recognizable capital G and E. Printing his initials on a legal form was a daunting task.

In 2005 and 2006, George's most notable behavior connected to reading and writing was his constant sifting through, stacking, and rearranging of the articles, offprints, and manuscript and typescript pages spread out on the window seat of our living room. These were all pieces he had written. There were dog-eared issues of periodicals that contain his essays. Here in *Partisan Review* #3, 1990, is his first essay, "The Pleasure of Its Being Over," which I remember he was working on in June 1989 when we had just come back from three months in France. In *Partisan Review* #4, 1991, is "Music and Postmodernism." In *Musical Quarterly*, Volume 75 #3, "The Nonsense of an Ending: Closure in Haydn's String Quartets." In *Southwest Review*, Autumn 1990, "Involuntary Affinities: New Music and Performance in the Twentieth Century." To *Haydn Studies*, a collection published by Cambridge University Press in 1998, George contributed a chapter whose title contained one of his beloved retrogrades, "Papa Doc's Recap Caper: Haydn and Temporal Dyslexia."

Between 1989 and about 1997, while busy teaching and composing, George wrote these and other trenchant, learned, and witty prose pieces about various aspects of classical and twentieth-century music. He also wrote several book reviews. Most of these pieces were published.

Early in 2005, I had our typist put all these essays, published and unpublished, on disc, since George's constant shuffling, piling and sifting made me fear that something would get irretrievably lost. A publisher was found, the process of preparing camera-ready copy was completed, and despite myriad delays, George's collected prose was published as a book by Scarecrow Press. He did not seem to understand that the piles of paper were no longer needed; his constant rearranging and fingering continued unabated. ("It's his job," said my sister.) The offprints and typescripts, the covers of the journals and of *Haydn Studies*, became grubby with wear.

Of the countless colorful minor characters to be found in the novels of Charles Dickens, characters often memorable because of some outrageous eccentricity, one of my favorites is Mr. Dick in *David Copperfield*. When David, still a little boy, runs away from his evil stepfather, Mr. Murdstone, he finds shelter in Dover with his great-aunt Betsey Trotwood. Miss Trotwood, herself no slouch in the eccentricity department, but staunchly good-hearted, turns out to have an unexplained gentleman known as Mr. Dick living with her. Even to naive young David, Mr. Dick seems very peculiar. Aunt Betsey claims, when she introduces David to Mr. Dick, that she relies on the latter's judgment; but it isn't many weeks before David finds the courage to ask his aunt whether Mr. Dick isn't slightly mad. Certainly not, is the answer. But Dickens, writing with a wonderfully tactful balance between child's-eye view and adult perception, soon makes it perfectly clear that there is something more than a bit odd about Mr. Dick.

Chief among Mr. Dick's benign eccentricities are his struggles with an unfinished and unfinishable Memorial, a lengthy memo he is permanently in the process of composing so as to submit it to some vaguely sketched authorities. Mr. Dick's endless hours spent fussing over this document were vividly evoked for me by George's chronic sifting through his manuscripts. Mr. Dick, we are told in one of those inimitable Dickens touches, makes "feeble efforts" to refrain from mentioning the head of King Charles I in his work in perpetual progress, but King Charles's head will not stay out of Mr. Dick's pages, and he further complains that "all the trouble has gotten out of his [the king's] head into mine." As recreation, Mr. Dick likes to construct kites made of "old leaves of abortive Memorials," and as the kite flutters to the ground, he "look[s] about him in a lost way."

Something about the hopeless, tentative mildness of this gentle and unforgettable character appealed to me even as a child when I first heard my half-brother David read *David Copperfield* aloud, but now I understand Mr. Dick much better. In his childlike dependency, his docility and passivity, his covering up of his confusion when asked a direct question, his surprising ability sometimes to give a sensible answer, and his obsessions and perseverations, he resembles George. And like George, Mr. Dick tends not to be quite diagnosable. We learn later that before being rescued by Miss Trotwood he had suffered a brain fever and been abandoned by his family. All this is well within the range of what George's situation could easily have been.

Had Dickens seen people with dementia? The question answers itself. The novels provide galleries of obsessive, sadistic, paranoid, traumatized, or otherwise damaged people ranging from mildly eccentric to psychotic or sociopathic. But Mr. Dick's eccentricities come at moments so close to George's endless fiddling with his drafts that I often wish the yellowing, dog-eared pages that litter our window seat could, like the false starts and discarded versions of Mr. Dick's Memorial, be made into a kite and, in a magical form of publication, "disseminating the statements pasted on" them, be flown high in the sky.

George's constant piling up and spreading out of what he has written bears the same relation to reading or writing as an artist's (that is, an artist who no longer paints) rearranging of the canvases in his studio bears to painting. Or I think of a sculptor who, losing his eyesight, fingers the statues he made years ago, statues that still keep him company in his studio. George's articles and his music (a CD is in the works): these are part of what is left of him, who he will eventually become.

Considering the debut volume of poetry by his recently deceased young friend Hans Lodeizen—hence a posthumous debut—James Merrill asked himself, "Wouldn't I too turn, word by word, page by page, into books on a shelf?" But such a transformation is both delayed and more confusing when the artist goes on living but is unable to make art.

George's *Collected Essays on Modern and Classical Music* was published in 2008. Reading and rereading this book, I constantly rediscover George's wit and brilliance; I am struck afresh by his thoughtfulness, his wide culture, and the elegance of his prose. Many of our conversations come back to me—a benefit I never anticipated as I doggedly saw the book through the press.

George is very proud of the book. Asked by neurologist number two in January 2007 how he spent his days, he answered, "I'm a composer," and added, "I have a book coming out." He keeps a copy in his room, and often puts it in his pocket when he goes out. He carries it around like a talisman.

CHAPTER 12

Around the Table

When I returned from the frontotemporal dementia conference in San Francisco in September 2006, I picked up the phone and called the John Hancock Company. It was time to see whether the long-term-care policy we had providentially bought a few years before would cover some household help for George. He was almost always at home; if I or our devoted housekeeper wasn't around, he was alone. Someone to come in and cook dinner, keep him company in the afternoons, to stay until I returned when I taught my evening seminar . . .

I now know that it often takes family caregivers a long time to get to the point of hiring outside help: everyone has to cross their own private Rubicon. As was typical for our situation, no clear line of demarcation presented itself to force my decision. George wasn't incontinent or violent; he didn't need to be lifted or washed; he was pretty much okay with what are known as the Activities of Daily Living. But he was essentially and increasingly incommunicado. If something had gone wrong while he was alone, it was far from certain that he would have known what to do, or that he'd have been able to do it even if he had known. He had avoided the telephone for years; I wasn't sure that he could understand what he read; he spoke less and less; it seemed to me that he understood less and less of what was said to him.

At that point, I was already well into the process of taking household decisions into my own hands. When I'd decided to go to San Francisco, I didn't tell George where I was going; when I returned, he didn't ask me where I'd been. When we began to have aides over to the apartment in the late afternoons, I told him it was because I knew he needed to eat a good dinner and I wasn't always around to cook it. I told him I needed more household help. He wasn't enthusiastic, but as I recall, he didn't protest; he certainly didn't ask many questions. As it turned out, the first aide we hired was not a very good cook, but she had some success getting George to teach her the moves of chess, and they used to take walks. Later aides were better cooks. It worked well enough, for a while.

Before George's benefits kicked in, though, we had to negotiate an intervening level of bureaucracy. In effect, George had to be examined for cognitive impairment; if he failed the mini-mental, then the insurance company could proceed. He failed with flying colors.

Being present at such Q and A sessions is no longer as startling for me as it used to be, though I always find something mesmerizing in an awful way, something almost voyeuristic or shameful, about sitting in on a scene that has its own kind of intimacy. But at the beginning, I was spellbound by every hesitant response, every flubbed answer.

So here we are: the red-haired, Australian visiting nurse, George, and I, sitting around the four-by-eight-foot table that almost filled my parents' dining room on Riverside Drive and after my mother's death took up residence in our dining room, where it has a bit more space. When I was small, I used to play house under this very table, or else simply crouch beneath it and hide, enjoying the illusion of invisibility. Now, on this brilliant late September morning fast turning into noon, I wish I could again crawl under this table and hide. On second thought, I am hiding—hiding in plain sight.

How does one do this? A common and instinctive technique is to not look anyone in the eye: if you can't see them, they can't see you. It would be good to be allowed to sit here with my eyes tight shut, or, maybe better still, with my head in my hands. Failing those options, I fix my gaze on an article about teaching *King Lear* in a community college. The article is on the table because the current issue of the periodical it appears in contains a poem of mine entitled "Rear Window"— a poem, come to think of it, about hiding in plain sight.

The nurse, who has been sent by the long-term-care insurance company, or rather by an intermediate outfit called Care-Scout, is sitting on my right. Her forearms are downy, almost hairy—"But in the lamplight, downed with light brown hair," as Prufrock observed of other arms on another occasion. But no lamplight is needed in this bright room at this hour. At the head of the table, where I usually sit, George is—one can't say presiding. Stony-faced, smoldering, he sits. He is angry, probably in part because he is getting bored and hungry, and in part because he is being annoyingly, humiliatingly, intrusively asked to know more than he can know; to remember more than he can remember. (In part, too, because his default mode these days is a dull anger.) My task at this table turns out to involve what is so often my role these days: to see, to register, to react to less, instead of more, than what's in front of my nose and screamingly visible.

Spell "world" backward. Subtract from one hundred by sevens. What year is this? If you needed help in the night, what would you do? Copy this figure of two intersecting pentagons. What day of the week is it?

This last one he knows: it's Friday. My first thought is that he's wrong: it's Saturday. It feels like Saturday, somehow. And this lopped, stretched, bisected day, what's left of it, which is quite a lot, goes on feeling like Saturday. But in fact he's right, I'm wrong: it's Friday. It follows, then—and here my mind can take a little walk—that all the sunny forenoon, only a few blocks away, on Ninety-seventh Street between Amsterdam and Columbus, the farmers' market is in full swing. Glowing orange pumpkins, squash, carrots; golden chrysanthemums; various greens of spinach, chard, kale, cabbage, leeks, parsley; reds of apples; vermilion tomatoes; eggs, honey, cheese, breads—autumn's cornucopia spilling over. And here around the big table the three of us sit.

Oh reason not the need.

I'm reminded of *King Lear*: the end of clarity, the loss of dignity, the pathos, the smacking up against merciless limits. But since this semester I am teaching another tragedy, I happen to be thinking more about it: *Hamlet*. The sudden (or imagined) changes blowing in and out like morphing clouds, camel to weasel to whale; the good and bad moments and days; the irretrievable obscurity of the condition, so that every statement is a question and all the questions are wrong. To be or not to be? Do you know me, my lord? What to me is this quintessence of dust? If Hamlet flunks his own mini-mental, it's surely on purpose. Isn't it?

In literature, says the article to which my gaze keeps sliding back and back as this inquisition continues, we are seldom fully aware of why it is we're moved. Oh, so we're fully aware of that in life? Well, sometimes we are. But it is not a consummation devoutly to be wished when a day, or a piece of a day, achieves as much clarity as this bright September forenoon bestows. I dreaded this time around the table; lo and behold, it turns out to be dreadful. But finally it is over, and George slams angrily out on one of his many daily walks. The nurse finishes her tea, and she and I finish our talk. Perhaps, if I hurry, I can still get to the farmers' market before it closes.

CHAPTER 13

Comfortably You Lie Back

When the weather was warm, in the fall and spring, George and I used to spend a lot of time, together and separately, walking in the park, or rather parks—he gravitated toward Central Park, I preferred Riverside Park. When the weather was right, I liked to go right down to the edge of the Hudson River and walk along Cherry Tree Walk. Usually I'd find a rock or jetty and sit there sunning myself, almost in the water. The sun and glare from the water made me sleepy, and I wasn't the only one. It was fun to watch other rock-sitters and sunbathers. Often, like me, they'd brought a book out to the river's edge, only to succumb to the spell of the sun.

When George accompanied me on these walks down to the river, as he often did in the spring of 2005 and 2006, and sometimes in 2007, he made no pretence of taking a book. He'd perch gracefully on a rock, smoking a cigarette and looking out at the sun, shimmering on the river or going down across the water. I'd sometimes lean against him. We didn't talk.

Drift

I love to spy what people
curled beside the river
are reading: Epictetus,
Fermat's Last Theorem, Madame Bovary

until the afternoon
sun has its way with them.
Broad and glaucous river;
weeds and glittering rocks;

a navy T-shirt someone
shat on; a broken bottle.
One reader on the bank
from squinting in the glare

has yielded to the hour
and drifted off downstream,
still there in basking body,
but dreaming, absent, gone.

You are like that:
your mind a mote shining across the water,
your person, handsome, lean,
elegantly angled to the sun.

Horizontality, water, light, sleep, waking: repeated unchallenging elements of a life. George's body somehow knew how to position itself even on a jagged boulder half-submerged in the dubious brown waters of the Hudson, and I could enjoy his enjoyment of the sun, the cigarette, the afternoon or evening light.

A similar sense of George's unimpaired physical well-being is touched on in "Bath," but this poem also expresses the disconnect between mind and body. In it, George's bath is not only the water in the tub but the disease inside his brain—an invisible bath there is no getting out of. George had always enjoyed bathing, lying back in the warm water. And it always seemed to me that there was something hopeful for us both in the way he used to climb out of the tub as if born afresh, emerging naked and clean, fresh and unimpaired, into the world—as if the bath water were an illness that, as he toweled off, could be drained away and left behind, consigned to a grubby memory.

Bath

Bath as in water. Here a bath of light,
daylong immersion, glare
shimmering and lapping through the shutters.
Memory of bath and bath of memory:
I dip in, get out, dry off, resubmerge.

Now that I am far away I see
clearly that your illness is a bath
in which you soak, then presently climb out.
In vain: this bath goes everywhere with you,
portable, inconspicuous,
the inner bath your brain is stewing in,
the bath they tested with the spinal tap.
You do not recognize that you are soaking.
Comfortably you lie back.

CHAPTER 14

A Kind of Goodbye

An early spring Sunday in 2007. One more day. Between breakfast and lunch—or is it between lunch and dinner?—George is lying on the bed waiting, maybe, for the next thing. He's wearing shorts and a T-shirt and sneakers, as if ready for tennis, but today isn't a tennis day. On these warm spring days, whenever he comes in from one of his many rapid walks, he puts on a clean T-shirt.

One hand rests on Erica, our cushiony orange cat. His eyes are fixed on—is it the ceiling? He hasn't shaved today—or yesterday or the day before. Does he still shave? As with other questions about abilities that seem to be on the way out (Does he still read? Does he still put on CDs?), the answer is: Sometimes. Occasionally. On the other hand, there are some questions (Does he still tackle the daily crossword puzzle? Does he still play the piano?) to which the answer is no.

In a rare impulse, I bend and kiss his bare, tanned knee. Why do I do this now, this time? It's a kind of goodbye, since I'm on my way out on one of my many rapid errands. Also, when I came into the bedroom to see if he was awake, it looked to me for a moment as if there were tears in his eyes.

Are there? I do not dare ask him. I hardly dare to look more closely. I don't want to know the answer; I don't want to suggest or supply or force or cue an answer. Above all, I don't want to set the stage for an argument, to worry or sadden him, or to stoke a conflict that would only anger me. The best outcome, if I did dare ask if he was crying and then ventured on to the scary part, the why, would be for me to lie down next to him on the bed and put my arms around him so we could both mourn. Or, more likely, I would—still lying next to him— mourn by myself. But I am not up to it.

So after kissing his knee, I straighten up, and then—backing out of the bedroom—I blow him a kiss. I try, for once, to trace his opaque pale blue gaze, to see where it's going and tug it down from there, as if the goal were for our eyes to meet. It doesn't happen. Yet often enough, his eyes follow me around a room, silently asking, "What now? What am I supposed to do?" Possibly they're asking something else: "What are you up to?" Or maybe they are asking nothing at all.

The blown kiss, as if one of us were standing on the deck of an ocean liner leaving for a long voyage—the blown kiss, the attempt to meet his eyes: these gestures, which under other circumstances might be a prelude to speech, boomerang back. Not that George thrusts me away; he's simply indifferent. I think. Still, for one split second, the pane of glass behind which he now lives seems to dissolve, like a windshield running with rain. Fleetingly I remember what the old connection felt like, back when I shared thoughts all day long with the person I lived with. But no sooner does the memory take shape than it fades, sinking back into the default of our days; yet it leaves a sharpened sense, almost a taste, of what has been lost. His loss, my loss, our loss.

These are the moments I think my heart will break. But it's impossible to overstate, not only how rapidly they vanish, but how tiny they are, how close to invisible, in relation to the scale of the life he and I are living day by day, the life we've been sliding into for how many years I can only estimate. Memories of the life before are like tiny bubbles on the grayish surface of a vast and tideless inland sea round and round which he and I are drifting. Or not a sea: a muddy river, ever so sluggishly bearing him away.

Get up and slither quickly into clothes and stride out to buy the paper. Breakfast. Walk. Nap or lie down. Snack. Sit or walk again, waiting for lunch. Lunch. Walk. Nap or TV (soccer or tennis), or maybe listen to a CD. Tuesdays and Thursdays, tennis with the trainer. On tennis days, a bath. Lie down. Walk. Wait for dinner. TV news, and dinner, and walk, and so—having uttered maybe fifty words on a chatty day—to bed.

Horizontality shared in sleep; his immobility; my scurrying; the sense of being becalmed, stuck . . . it may have been early in 2007 that I stirred these ingredients of daily life into a villanelle.

The Boat

All day I bustle in and out
While you're at home. No, far away.
All night we sail in the same boat.

I think of trying to invite
Friends whom we no longer see.
All day I'm busy—in and out.

For you the hours accumulate
Or fly by, maybe—don't ask me.
At night we sail in the same boat.

The ties that bind have grown too tight.
Entangled, you sit peacefully;
I squirm and struggle to get out.

Angry, impatient, or contrite,
I stir the pot of poetry.
At night we idle in our boat.

To lose a self without a fight . . .
You barely have a word to say.
My mind's revolving, in and out.
Nights we sail blindly in our boat.

CHAPTER 15

So Long Without Loving

I think I am forgetting how to talk.

We've eaten dinner early, as usual. It's the middle of May 2007; the days are long, and the sun is only now beginning to get low. In November and December, George often went to bed at six-thirty or seven, but this evening it's too light for even him to think of bed yet. So I suggest a walk in Riverside Park, and out we go.

As we stride along unspeaking, I remember that I woke up at five this morning after a bad dream and then went back to sleep. As often seems the case with my dawn dreams, this one felt true; but I can't remember what it was about. On we walk, not talking.

Last week I taught the semester's final seminar in my poetry graduate course. This particular class was devoted to James Merrill. Somehow, unless it was my wishful thinking rather than an accurate observation, the students all seemed to rise to the level of articulate civility, of alertness and ingenuity, that characterized Merrill as a social presence during his lifetime and that indelibly distinguish his work as well.

The poem we happened to spend the most time on in that last class was "Days of 1964." Until I reread it for the course, I hadn't thought about that piece in several years; and as often happens with good poems after a hiatus, it struck me now with fresh force. Not only was "Days of 1964" still moving, many-layered, and beautiful, but like many of the poems that had been coming to my aid since George's illness had begun to change our lives, it seemed weirdly apposite. "Days of 1964" reminisces about a time (obviously), a place, and a love affair; and it is also about love itself or rather, since the poem has a distinctly allegorical tenor, I should say about Love.

Why, in this difficult spring, would a love poem speak to me so urgently? Maybe because the poem was filling what my father used to enjoy calling a much needed gap. For quite a while now, love had been in short supply.

When poems speak to me freshly, I notice lines that somehow passed me by before, or I read familiar lines with a new emphasis. For me, in that final seminar, it was the last stanzas of "Days of 1964" that bloomed like a lavish new flower, especially the lines I italicize.

> Forgive me if you read this. (And may Kyria Kleo,
> Should someone ever put it into Greek
> And read it aloud to her, forgive me, too.)
> *I had gone so long without loving,*
> *I hardly knew what I was thinking.*
>
> Where I hid my face, your touch, quick, merciful,
> Blindfolded me. A god breathed from my lips.
> *If that was illusion, I wanted it to last long;*
> To dwell, for its daily pittance, with us there,
> Cleaning and watering, sighing with love or pain . . .

The speaker apologizes to the lover who has occasioned the poem. He asks forgiveness not only for telling an indiscreet anecdote about Kleo, the cleaning lady, but also for some of his own trains of thought or fantasy. In addition, he ruefully justifies himself for any extravagant behavior on the grounds that he hasn't been in his right mind—has, indeed, been possessed ("A god breathed from my lips"). And the reason for this giddiness: "I had gone so long without loving, / I hardly knew what I was thinking."

The love affair that serves as the poem's occasion, theme, and backdrop has blown in like a rainstorm after a long drought—the whole neighborhood, we're told at the outset, is "trembling still / In pools of the night's rain"—and it has left the speaker, as he puts it toward the end of the poem, "falling, legs / Buckling, heights, depths, / Into a pool of each night's rain." Eros has swept all reason out of his head, a state of affairs that is fine with him: "If that was illusion, I wanted it to last long."

Somehow, I'd never before caught the note of screwball comedy in that line—its charming, willed, knowing, love-struck goofiness. If I was besotted, the speaker concedes, it's partly because I wanted to be; if I was living in a fool's paradise, I wanted to stay there as long as I could. Besides, that "if" raises the possibility of a contrary-to-fact clause; maybe it wasn't illusion at all. Maybe, just maybe, and for however long or short a time it lasted, this love was the real thing.

In May 2007, those were the parts of this poem that reached out to me. They didn't apply with much logic or precision to my own life; the words didn't quite fit, but the tune was right. The thirst, the loneliness, the habituation to emotional deprivation that marked the way I was living. . . . Somewhere, there are pools of rain, ardor, and longing. Somewhere there is joy—illusory, maybe, but you want it to last.

I didn't know what I wanted. I knew what I didn't want. I didn't want to go on living in this cage of silence, this dumb desert, with a man who no longer spoke to me. I had gone so long living in this deepening drought that I hardly noticed it any more. I didn't visit my own thoughts much, until poems and dreams brought me face to face with them.

George and I walk on. As usual, I have to speed up a little to keep up with him. Nearly everyone who walks with him does; he is almost six foot four, and he doesn't slow down for companions. I try to remember what it was like walking with him in this park when Jonathan was tiny. We would each hold one of our son's hands, count to three, and swing him, and he'd squeal with glee. Surely George must have slowed down then, to keep pace with the stride of a little boy. When he hoisted Jon onto his shoulders, our son rode at a kingly height. Now Jon is almost six foot three himself.

May in Riverside Park. The leaves have lost the bright yellowish-green gloss of April and are now so deep a green that they appear nearly blue. They look damp, a little swollen. We stride north to about 110th Street, then turn back south, walk down to 100th Street, and climb the steps to the Firemen's Monument.

The monument, with its large formal fountain backed by a bas-relief bronze sculpture of horse-drawn fire engines, is inextricably connected in my mind with the history of George's and my last few years. For one thing, it was George's nightly destination for his postprandial cigarette walks, which began, I think, as long ago as the fall of 2000. He would stroll from our apartment on 101st Street and West End Avenue to the monument at 100th and Riverside Drive.

Were his deepening silence and these regular walks the only changes I noticed back then? For a while, maybe. Sometimes I'd accompany him on these walks, or even have a cigarette myself to keep him company, but these cigarette walks weren't signs of intimacy. They were rituals, and they took place, unless I made some conversation, in almost total silence. It was as if by joining George on his walks I was trying to get closer to him by edging into the opaque realm of his silence.

Life went on, as it does. He didn't tell me he was having trouble teaching; but then I didn't ask. Fast forward to the fall of 2001. On Monday, September 10, I came home tired but jubilant after teaching my first graduate class of the semester—class had gone well; I felt revved up. There was no dinner waiting for me, and not much in the way of welcome (did he get off the sofa?), but I had gotten used to that. *I had gone so long without loving, / I hardly knew what I was thinking.*

I filled the usual silence by talking about my class, and my enthusiasm, or something I said, angered George. We had an argument, of which all I remember is his phrase, "You were loaded for bear," as if I'd come home spoiling for a fight. I assume my pleasure in teaching seemed like a reproach or rebuke to him, but maybe his anger was kindled by my rapid speech. Maybe I'd had the nerve to comment that I was hungry. Maybe what irked him was nothing at all, or nothing he could recognize.

I wouldn't even remember this minor squabble were it not that the next day was September 11. Now that I do think back to that evening, though, it fits right into the pattern I've been accumulating, piece by piece—a pattern like a path through the woods, a trail whose beginning you can't quite remember.

In the terrifying time after 9/11, it seemed reassuring that our little family was intact. Public events, no matter how unsettling, were something to talk about, to watch on TV. Jonathan was a senior in high school, and there was college to be thought of. George took Jon to visit Oberlin, his alma mater, though I bought the tickets, arranged the motel, the airport car, all the details. It was George's last airplane flight.

In the evenings that fall, he'd take his cigarette walk to the Firemen's Monument. Quite often, I'd still accompany him. The autumn nights were mild and brilliant; the leaves of the sycamore trees, illuminated by the streetlights, were green and brown tinged with gold. In the weeks after 9/11, the great basin of the fountain at the monument was heaped high with flowers. We weren't the only visitors to what had become a shrine, one of many in the grieving city. And again, our evening silences felt, for a while, companionable, cozy. So what if there wasn't much to say? We'd had years of talking to each other in the past, I told myself. We'd have years more in the future. Did I say that about the future to myself? If I said it, did I believe it?

Over the next few years, the semi-companionable silence withered away. Pieces of the accumulating pattern, steps on the winding path: all are visible only in retrospect. Jonathan went off to college. How many times did I give George our son's cell phone number and encourage him to call Jon? George was sinking deeper into silence, but still teaching, after some fashion; still reading the paper; still playing the piano. I was busy teaching and writing. Life retained its general shape, even if something was draining out of it. Looking at my journals from those years, 2002, 2003, I see sentences like "Worried about George," after which I zoom away to other topics. *I had gone so long without loving, / I hardly knew what I was thinking.*

In the spring of 2004, George was on leave, and he went down to the Virginia Center for the Creative Arts. I bought his train ticket down; but there were problems of some sort, a month later, with his return ticket, which I hadn't bought. He'd thought he had a train reservation back to New York but had misunderstood or otherwise mishandled matters, and he had no reservation. Angry and worried, he called me at five in the morning on the day he was to come home. Later that day he got a ride back to the city with another colonist. Whatever time I thought he might arrive, he came many hours later; waiting for him was a long nightmare. He never called to tell me they were delayed by traffic; probably he couldn't use cell or pay phones, or lacked cash. Presumably it was because he had no cash that, when they finally arrived in Soho, he took the subway home with his huge bag. But he may already have been avoiding what taxi rides require: mental arithmetic, and conversations with a stranger.

Never once in all this time did he admit to having any trouble or ask for help.

Now on this green May evening in 2007, the silence in which George and I have been lapped for years has gone dry and brittle. True, it does dissipate some when we go outside, like stale air when you open a window. So why, I ask myself reproachfully, do we not take walks in the park every nice day? How hard can it be to trot beside him, or to sit next to him and his silence on a bench? The best answer I can come up with is: It can be hard. It is hard.

Here we are, back at the Firemen's Monument, completing the loop on our homeward walk. Others are also sitting, singly or in groups, on the marble benches. One man is reading a book; another is smoking a cigar. A dog frisks on its leash— it wants to splash in the fountain. George and I are one more couple enjoying the green of early evening, and it is cruel of me not to do this, not to want to do it, not to be able to bear to do it, every day.

If that was illusion, I wanted it to last long. But where this Merrillian wish has a daffy gusto, my life with George, skeletal, stripped dry, is no illusion. It is what our marriage has become, and it may go on like this, regardless of my wishes and needs, for decades. Unless I take a step to end it, unless I take some decisive step.

Now this morning's dream comes back to me. My son, one of his friends, and I are lost without a map in the wilderness. Are we in a car? A small plane? The windows are rolled up; water presses against the panes, murky greenish-gray water, and it's rising. Soon it will be over our heads. I start to say something sententious to the young men, as if I were launching into a lecture. On the point of drowning, a lecture? And then I woke up.

No sooner do I recall the dream than the sense of panic and crisis goes back undercover. Everything is mild and soft and normal. Here I am sitting on a tepid marble bench beside the man I've been married to for nearly thirty years. The tail of a dawn dream came; it went. The long gray day, the walk, the soft light; the illusion, so hard to shake, of a normal married life, if there is such a thing. *If that was illusion, I wanted it to . . .* to what? What do I want?

And look! A cardinal has just alighted on the rim of the fountain. I touch George's wrist to get his attention, and point—all this without words.

CHAPTER 16

Backups

In July 2007, to give me a break, Jonathan devised a scheme: George would spend a few weeks with Jon and a few of his friends on a Vermont hilltop. Not our hilltop, though we have a house on a hill in Vermont; this place was more of an encampment than a house, and some of the group had been there since May.

With most of these young men, all friends from Swarthmore, Jon had spent much of the previous year in Missoula, Montana; their numbers had fluctuated, but I'd thought of them as the Missoula Seven. Now in this new venue I would think of them as—what? There being no electricity on the hilltop, the boys (if it's allowed to refer to twenty-three- and twenty-four-year-olds as boys) used the Chelsea Public Library, a few miles away, for the Internet. And the post-office box some of them rented was in the hamlet of Washington, a bit closer in the other direction on Route 110. But prosaic labels like the Chelsea Four or the Washington Five weren't right.

It turned out that the hilltop compound, with its pond and apple trees and vegetable garden, its cabins and barn and outhouse, its pens for pigs, goats, and chickens, was called by its inhabitants—and had been so called, I gathered, since its founding as a commune around 1970 by the father of one of the current inhabitants—Prospero's Island. This name conveys the poetry of the place, though I found I'd been imagining the settlement less as a Shakespearean isle than as a Hesiodic mountainside. Perhaps my prolonged project of co-editing an anthology of Greek poetry in translation made me think of Jonathan and his friends' enterprise in terms of the poet Hesiod pasturing his flock on Mount Helicon. What they were undertaking to do up there with George was, as I phrased it to myself, pastoral therapy. The pastoral component of this label did justice to the livestock, the gardens, and the hilltop. And the therapy part? The Homeric noun *therapon* means a servitor or squire; the sense of a cure associated with such service, *therapeia*, came later perhaps, but the notion of therapy seemed wholly appropriate to the proposed setup.

To Prospero's Island, or Hesiod's Hillside, then, Jon would take his father early in July, and would, with his group of resident friends, look after him there, while I finished teaching two courses, flew to Athens, spent two weeks in Greece, and wound up my respite with a week alone back in New York, before heading up to Vermont to take George off the young men's hands. That was the plan.

Spending time in George's grave, almost silent presence reminds anyone who tries it how much we constantly depend on the music, or even the background noise, of speech, and on the play of facial expression. Jon and his floating circus of companions were undertaking to carry this oddly spectral burden for a while: to keep George company, make sure he ate well, didn't wander off the hilltop. Perhaps they'd be able to find him a few simple chores to do—turn the compost, pet the goats, feed the chickens. What, asked Jon, could go wrong?

All this sounds like the perfect recipe for a tale of catastrophe, some veritable Blair Witch Project narrative of well-meaning plans gone horribly awry. At the very least, the scheme might seem likely to lead to a comedy of mishaps and errors—George getting lost in the woods, for example—with a happy ending. No good deed goes unpunished; the best-laid plans are liable to failure. In fact, such is not the story I'm telling here. Even if our little scheme had failed, its failure would not have been my topic. What I find fascinating, looking back now on that summer, is something else—the nervous notion of backups as it arose in the double context of this pastoral scenario and a recent performance of *Hamlet*.

The concept of backups probably should have occurred to me and Jonathan when we started planning George's interlude on the hilltop, but the first person to raise the issue was George's young neurologist, who thought of it as soon as I mentioned the scheme. He approved of the plan in principle, but warned, "You know, you need a backup plan—and a backup for the backup." He was envisioning George wandering off and getting lost, or spraining an ankle, or being bitten by a snake, or at the very least becoming fearful or disoriented or angry. Jonathan and I could imagine these things too; we just didn't think they were very likely to happen. Still, to be on the safe side, I typed up some instructions for the hilltop gang and any doctor George might have occasion to see. Once the plan was put into action, after Jon and one of his friends had swooped down to the city, scooped up George, and driven him to Vermont, I found that I wasn't worrying at all.

Nevertheless, I must have kept the neurologist's admonition tucked away somewhere in my mind, for an unexpected echo of his words rang in my ears only a few days before I returned to Vermont—unexpected and also not, for in the past few years it has become a frequent occurrence for a chance remark or a line from a well-known poem to strike a familiar chord. The source of this latest echo was *Hamlet*. This seems appropriate, for the play is an inexhaustible literary trove—a trove, moreover, that I had taught for an entire semester the previous fall. But the particular node of meaning in the play this time around was something that in previous encounters with *Hamlet* I had always managed to miss.

Still jetlagged from the flight home from Greece, I happened to pass, as I drifted sleepily along Broadway, a poster announcing a neighborhood production of *Hamlet*. The fifteen-dollar ticket and the venue (a church) were irresistible, so I took myself to a performance of the Frog & Peach Theater's *Hamlet*.

My expectations weren't high. Even so, the start of the play, after a prolonged and unexplained delay, was a definite disappointment: too many cuts made in the early scenes, and mediocre acting. I thought of leaving at intermission. But something made me stick around, partly inertia, no doubt, but partly also the thoughtful performance of the actor who played Claudius. He doubled quite effectively as the Ghost by putting on gauntlets, transforming his gait to a stagger, and rolling his eyes; but as Claudius he got my attention, and so I stayed.

By the time we reached Act 4, the director seemed to have tired of cutting—or the play's momentum had taken over. In a scene that I remembered, though the details of this particular speech had faded somewhat (perhaps because they are often cut in performance), Claudius excelled, reciting his lines as if he were thinking aloud, plotting along step by step, trying hard and successfully—no dysexecutive personality he—to anticipate the next obstacle.

Act 4, Scene 7: Claudius and Laertes are plotting the murder of the man they have different reasons for detesting. Claudius suggests that in the proposed fencing match Hamlet be stabbed with a bare foil ("a sword unbated"), and Laertes, with nary a pause for breath or a break in the rhythm, agrees and elaborates, rejoining, "I will do't, / And for that purpose I'll anoint my sword."

But this clever backup, the sword not only unbated but poisoned, is not enough for Claudius. With a canny thoroughness the neurologist would surely have applauded, the King promptly thinks another step ahead to what might happen if both components of the sword plan should fall through:

> Let's further think of this,
> Weigh what convenience both of time and means

> May fit us to our shape. If this should fail,
> And that our drift look through our bad performance,
> 'Twere better not assayed; therefore this project
> Should have a back or second, that might hold
> If this did blast in proof. Soft, let me see . . .

And indeed, only one more line interposes before Claudius arrives at the backup for the backup—"I ha't!" What he has now come up with is the poisoned pearl ready to be dropped into the goblet that the thirsty Hamlet—"When in your motion you are hot and dry, / As make your bouts more violent to that end"—will surely want to swig from.

We know how it turns out. The backups all work—work all too well, in fact, for the chain reaction of victims speedily gets out of hand, resulting in a stage littered with corpses. Each victim of the careering plot figures out, just as he or she realizes that his or her own death is imminent, the relevant piece of the scheme: "The point envenomed too?" "The drink, the drink!"

"Purposes mistook / Fall'n on the inventors' heads," as Horatio—who is given the challenging task of reporting Hamlet's "cause aright / to the unsatisfied"—aptly puts it. Earlier in the play, Hamlet has sardonically described the fate he plans for Rosencrantz and Guildenstern in similar terms, whose aptness will extend farther than the speaker can know: "For 'tis the sport to see the engineer / Hoist with his own petard."

Are there too many backups in *Hamlet*, or do they work too well? Tragedy invites what-ifs: Suppose the sword had been unabated but not poisoned? What if the Queen had not drunk from the poisoned cup? The redundancy of Claudius and Laertes' scheme is dramatized when the dying Hamlet forces the King, whom he has just stabbed with the poisoned sword, to drink from the poisoned cup. The Prince thereby enacts his own backup (improvised and superfluous, to be sure, but still a backup), which functions to balance, belatedly, his accumulated delays.

The hinge connecting Elsinore with the hilltop in Vermont was this notion of backup. The neurologist, like Claudius, was trying to think ahead, encouraging me to encourage Jonathan and company to be ready for any contingency. I did my best to follow the doctor's suggestions. "Oh, I have a backup plan," I assured him. But my backup plan was as mild as milk, a matter of phone numbers, prescriptions, and medical records. The worst-case scenario was that should George for some reason prove unable to stay on the hilltop, then Jon would move him to our own Vermont house, and if that failed, he would take him home to the city, where our housekeeper ("a back or second") would hold down the fort until I returned from Greece.

Nothing went wrong. George never got lost in the woods; he didn't even get a mosquito bite. Without so much as an exasperated sigh at the anticlimactic absence of any emergency, July meekly went belly-up. Just as August was about to take its place, I arrived in Vermont right on schedule; right on schedule Jon delivered his father safe and sound, a bit dazed but tanned and newly bearded, back into my keeping. Life, in short, went on without any apparent need for a backup. But isn't that what backups are for: so that having put them in place, we can comfortably (and more often than not correctly) assume they won't be needed?

In the world of dementia, unlike the zero-sum game of co-vert murder, the absence of failure does not spell success. Still, his Hesiodic therapy had evidently been mildly pleasant for George, who said when asked that he had enjoyed the young men's company and that the food had been good. How about the goats—had he liked them? "There were a lot of them," he said vaguely. (There were four.)

For me the pastoral interlude provided a pair of gifts. First, two weeks in another place, another life really, with a different cast of characters—time during which, remarkably, I had been perfectly confident that all was well on the hilltop. I'd sat in for a week on my friend Alicia Stallings's superb poetry workshop on the island of Spetses in the Saronic Gulf. The other students—American, British, Canadian, Australian—ranged in age from undergraduate to older than I was. We all wrote every day; three of the poems in this book, "Bath," "The Flickering Reunion," and "Hotel," were written during that time. In the mornings, class met in a cool, marble-floored room a few blocks up the hill from the gleaming waterfront. I stayed with Alicia, her husband, and her young son in a house whose landlady, presiding in her shady courtyard with its grape arbor and wealth of potted plants, reminded Alicia of Calypso in her grotto. There were early morning swims, afternoon siestas, evening poetry readings as the sun went down and the moon rose over the harbor, and dinners at a *taverna* a few feet from the Aegean that began at 10:30 and went late into the night, everyone a little drunk with sun and poetry and retsina. After the Spetses session was over, I caught a ferry to Samos, the island where I had lived in the early 1970s. My two or three days alone in a little room back in the fishing village of Ormos, back in the Greek language, among people many of whom remembered me, as I remembered them (what was a mere thirty years or so?), was my own pastoral interlude that summer. This time wasn't just vacation, restorative R & R; it was a reclamation of a piece of my past.

And second, my chance evening at *Hamlet*, in which one actor's strong performance, in conjunction with the neurologist's admonitions, had memorably sharpened my sense of Claudius, that epitome of shrewd planning, as he fluently foresees and sketches out for his callower co-conspirator possibilities, behaviors, and contingencies, plots the backup for the backup for the backup. How executive he is. How fail-safe his schemes. And see how it ends.

CHAPTER 17

The Spell

Not long after the Prospero's Island interlude was over and George and I were installed in our own house in Vermont, I went to see the film *Stardust*, fittingly playing at the Star Theater in St. Johnsbury. I like to go to at least one movie each summer at the Star, the theater which through various permutations (it certainly didn't use to be a triplex) has remained in the same spot on Eastern Avenue for as long as I've spent summers in the vicinity, which is a very long time. A year or two before, I'd enjoyed reading *Stardust*, a fairy tale of sorts by the gifted fantasist Neil Gaiman. Since I'd taken the book out of the Northeast Vermont Regional Library, which is located at the end of our dirt road, a feeling of summer hung for me over both the book and the film.

Other feelings the film aroused were less benign. Faithful to the text, the film of *Stardust* stresses transformation as both plot device and theme. Boy into billy goat, old hag into young beauty, hero into mouse . . . most of the transformations are reversible, after the time-honored manner of fairy tales. Still, the fear that a transformation can't be undone, perhaps more vivid in the film than the book, recalls the vengeful and often frightening transformations so frequent in Ovid's *Metamorphoses*. Both in Ovid and in Gaiman, to transform someone into, say, an animal is a blatant display of power and often of malice.

What especially struck me in the film was the fact that not only did the transformed victim's human shape disappear, so did his or her power of speech. Ovid often stresses the removal of the victim's ability to speak, sometimes to humorous effect, as with Io's mooing, but the speechlessness of Actaeon as a stag or Daphne as a laurel tree is poignant, pathetic, and chilling. In the film, I especially noticed a merchant who after the wave of a witch's wand could only cheep like a bird, though he retained his human shape. I think it was this deceptively unchanged outer aspect that gave me the idea of a slow transformation, such that the waved wand's effect, though devastating, is invisible at any given moment. Of course the abracadabra of the magic spell is lightning-swift, while the slow transformation is what time does to all of us. The transformation wrought by dementia isn't invariably slow. Still, very often the deficits manifest gradually.

A poem I wrote after seeing *Stardust*, entitled "The Spell," focuses on one striking aspect of cognitive decline. It takes up the notion of a gradual and invisible transformation, which slowly erases the victim's power of speech.

The Spell

A wand waved, slow and sly,
Imposed a creeping chill,
Blighted wish and will
So he could not say "I."

Yes, your wish has been heard.
Unbroken peace will reign.
Your husband will remain
But scarcely ever utter one more word.

You longed to enter his walled garden and
Have no rivals—such was your command?
So be it. No one now disputes your claim
To live with him, to feed and care for him.

Within that garden henceforth, on each road,
Yours is the bearing of his lonely load.

As well as the notion of a spell, this poem recycles a simile I'd come up with many years before when I was first telling my shrink about George, the fascinating new man in my life. He seems, I said, to live inside a walled garden—a place to which I want to gain access.

Be careful what you wish for. The shared, rapt silence, first at the MacDowell Colony and later in Vermont: here was a tranquil garden, a charmed circle to which I did indeed gain access. But to go on living, year after year, with someone who is being slowly walled in by silence? To keep him company, as the walls rise higher and higher, inside that more and more restricted and isolated space?

The walled garden, the wish granted, the cruel spell: here was the world of fairy tales, a world whose cruelty and violence, as well as excitement and beauty, Gaiman's story brings vividly to life. In this world (and certainly in the film version of *Stardust*), the villains and witches are often more memorable than the hero and heroine. In my poem, the cruelty is there, all right, but seems to lack agency. Who waves the wand of dementia? I take refuge in the passive voice: the wand is waved.

One of the most common complaints of the people in both the support groups I've been attending is that we're mentally overwhelmed. When the person you're caring for is suffering from an ailment that affects cognition, there's twice as much to remember, to know, to keep track of. One's own constantly accumulating store of memories gets progressively harder to contain as time passes; so how do you carry someone else's memories?

One More Thought

I had to carry it on your behalf.
But there was always something else to do.
I had to fear, remember, and imagine,
but there was always someplace else to go.

I had to bear it all for you. For me.
Throw this out and keep that. Forget and know.
Old jokes, old anecdotes
struggle to the surface even now.

Our neighbors at the movies holding hands.
Another bubble burst. The tears went dry.
What slowly leaked away through secret channels:
The person who said "I."

One more word about that lonely load I'm carrying in "The Spell." Flash back to January 2007: I've taken George to consult a specialist in Philadelphia. After numerous tests, he, I, and a social worker are straggling down a long, long hospital corridor. The spinal tap, the MRI are over; at long last we're on our way out of there. I have both our winter coats slung over one arm and an overnight bag on the other.

"Can I carry something for you?" asks the social worker as I flounder along, George stalking somewhere behind or in front, ignoring us. *L'esprit de l'escalier*, the answer I should have made, occurs to me only later: "Could you please carry my husband for a year or two?"

The lonely load is he. Is his. Is mine.

CHAPTER 18

In the Park

Fall 2007, back in the city. Tuesday, September 25 seemed like a pretty good day, to start with—one of those days when George was able to do more than I'd expected he could. More precisely, he was able do one of the things (there's a lengthening list of them) I had been assuming he no longer could do, or at least that he no longer did do. He cashed a check.

The last time I'd gone with him to the bank, I'd ascertained that his bank card was out of date. That problem, when I took him to the service desk and explained it, had been solved without too much difficulty. Today, with his new bank card in his wallet, and a check where he'd written his PIN number on the "Memo" line, he went to the bank alone. True, I'd asked him before he left the apartment if I could see the check he'd written. (I try not to hang over him when he writes.) He'd filled in everything correctly except the date, which he'd left blank. Slowly and carefully I told him the date, and slowly and carefully he wrote it on the check.

So he went to the bank and cashed his check for fifty dollars. Would this turn out to have been a modest achievement, an isolated incident, or the forerunner of future successes or problems? Suppose, now he had a valid bank card, he took to cashing a check every day—would that mean his buying a six-pack of beer every day? I was so tired of buying beer that I didn't drink that I had just about stopped doing it.

Well, time would tell. And what time told was that he didn't cash a check again. Like so much else, this incident proved to be isolated.

I didn't teach on Tuesdays, and that day I had been invited out to lunch. My new acquaintance, Arnold, a poet I had met in Greece that July, was visiting the city from his cabin in Maine. He was staying with his brother, Jerry, in a penthouse apartment in the Normandy, a building I had passed countless times on Riverside Drive but had never set foot in. The three of us—Arnold, the country mouse, Jerry, the city mouse, and I—had sandwiches on the terrace. The autumn day was clear and just warm enough. What a view! From where we sat, we couldn't see the river; our vista was to the east, so the Hudson was at our backs. But there were wonderful glimpses of rooftop gardens, other penthouse terraces, all sparkling in the sunny, slightly smoky air.

Up there, far above the traffic and the sidewalks, closer to the sky, it was easy to feel a sense of relief, release, perspective, as if this bird's-eye view somehow bestowed wisdom and detachment upon me; as if I'd risen above the mundane level of my troubles, instead of simply riding an elevator up to a penthouse. Yet this relief and release were really no different from the sensations I felt whenever I left our apartment.

Lunch done, I was back home in plenty of time to remind George that he had a four-thirty tennis date in the park with his trainer. Times, I had come to realize, were among the most challenging things for him to remember, so I tried to schedule tennis for days when I'd be around. Usually when he knew he had a tennis date, he'd get out his racket and a can of balls and leave them on the dining room table, or on an armchair, as a visible reminder. Then, as if the racket and balls were an issue of *Musical Quarterly* or *Partisan Review*, he'd often move them from one place to another—the coffee table, another armchair, the window seat.

Just in case I was delayed returning from lunch, I'd left several notes reminding him about his tennis—one on the bedside table, one on the dining room table, probably a third on the coffee table. (I was still leaving him notes then, though I'd stopped leaving him a daily schedule.) But he hadn't yet left the apartment when I got home. This was good; he often left an hour or more before the appointed time. Since the day was still beautiful, I decided to stroll along with him down to the courts by the river. I brought a book; and my plan was to sit in the sun on one of the benches near the courts while we waited for the trainer, an arrangement that had worked before.

As we left our apartment, though, things started to get slightly strange. When we walked out of our building on the corner of West End Avenue and 101st Street to go to Riverside Park, it was our habit to turn left and head south past Ansche Chesed Synagogue to 100th Street. But this time, as soon as we left our apartment building, George wanted to turn right, or north. This meant that we crossed West End Avenue at 101st Street instead of 100th. Admittedly, this was a very minor difference. Once in Riverside Park, he knew to turn south, and the new route involved less than one extra block to walk to get to the park. Still, this unexplained change in route and routine made no sense to me. We'd always gone the other, shorter way; and harmony lay precisely in habit. The fabric of our days was woven from routine.

Foolishly, perversely, because I must have known the effort was doomed to fail, I asked George why we were taking this new route. Nine times out of ten I would have gone along, trotting to keep up with him, in silence; but this must have been the tenth time.

"Why are we going this way, honey?" I asked. "We usually go by way of One Hundredth Street, remember?"

No answer.

Why did I even bother to ask? Maybe because an impatience had been building up in me in the few weeks since we'd returned from Vermont. That seems an arbitrary line to cross, though. An impatience had been building up in me a lot longer than that. Perhaps I was spoiling for a fight. Perhaps, tired of our tacit Don't Ask/Don't Tell policy, I thought I'd try to get a real answer if I could. Did I actually think that asking a question would earn me an answer? Maybe I was just idly, impulsively experimenting. I didn't get an answer, and I didn't get a fight either.

"Why are we going this way?" I almost yelled.

By now we'd crossed into Riverside Park and were walking south, toward the stairs at the lower level—our usual approach once we were in the park.

No answer.

I persisted: "I'm talking to you, dammit!"—except, evidently, I wasn't. On he strode. As usual, though I'm a pretty fast walker, it was an effort for me to keep up with him.

"George, please answer me when I speak to you. I just want to know why we went this way," I whined.

By now, of course, I no longer expected any response, if I ever had. But confusingly, at about this point in our non-conversation he nodded or shook his head—I can't remember which—or said Yes or No, some word perhaps intended to reassure me that he knew where he was going (as indeed he did). It wasn't an answer; it was a fleeting monosyllable or gesture, and I didn't understand what it meant, but maybe it was an attempt at a response.

Soon enough, anyway, there we were at the courts. My question had never been answered or even, other than this gesture/monosyllable, acknowledged. I am not sure George heard the question, though "heard" is not precisely the right verb for this particular cognitive problem. His trouble answering questions seemed to stem not only, or not so much, from not knowing the answer as from not understanding the question.

Some flaw in neural wiring made him essentially oblivious to questions as soon as they were uttered. So the questioner had these choices: fruitlessly repeat the question; answer it herself; or give up and join him in his silence.

"I can't read your mind, you know!" I barked at him sometimes. More often, I joined him on his narrow ledge of silence—a ledge that sometimes felt like a safe, if not terribly hospitable, place to perch, and at other times seemed, in the words of Thom Gunn's poem "Lament," "as restful as a knife."

CHAPTER 19

The Pack

_____

Fall 2007. I had come home from some errand or other; it was midmorning. George was pacing around the apartment looking unhappy. Maybe Mandy, our housekeeper, was late with his fruit shake and he was hungry—who knew? I couldn't read his mind. Mandy was better at it: "He's angry because the toast was burned," she'd say, or "He doesn't like the noise of the vacuum cleaner," much as she'd interpret the huffy moods of our unaccountable cat Erica.

Anyway, I noticed he looked unhappy. And an impatient impulse, or perhaps some maternal instinct gone stale, made me respond to his long face with a question. I should have known this was not a useful ploy.

"What's the matter?" I asked.

This time, though, he answered. "They pitched into me."

"Pitched into you? What do you mean?"

No answer.

"Honey, *who* pitched into you?"

With an effort, he got two words out: "The pack."

"The pack pitched into you? George, I don't know what you're talking about. Can you explain who did what?"

I tried to read his mind; to recreate the scene, if there had been one, from this scanty clue. Was he referring to a failed interaction at the bank or the store? Had there been a problem he couldn't solve, a difficulty involving money? Had someone said something to humiliate him? Or had it all been a figment, like the Namibia caper?

A year and a half before, back in December 2005, Columbia had put on a retirement concert for George, a selection of his chamber pieces. The concert had gone very well: wonderful performances of his difficult, delicate music; good attendance; a nice reception afterward in the lobby of Miller Theatre. I remember him surrounded by well-wishers, talking and laughing.

Then began our wait to receive the recording of this event. It was winter break, and the graduate student who was responsible for making the CD had gone to Namibia on safari with his parents (I think that was the story). January 2006 came and went; the spring semester began. Eventually, after many weeks of silence, word came from the embarrassed conductor that the graduate student had unaccountably pressed the wrong button, and no recording had been made.

There was no point arguing, though I came to feel there was a grain of truth in George's view that this mishap was really the result of a conspiracy. Even paranoids, after all, have enemies. Things had gone inexcusably wrong with what should have been a routine recording of this one-time-only concert, and no one was able to offer us a cogent explanation of why. Well, things had been going mysteriously wrong for George at Columbia, and elsewhere, for quite a while; this incident was merely more of the same. George's mordant humor was in evidence, lending a kind of familiarity to his confabulation. "Our man in Namibia," he'd say, rolling his eyes.

Not that the Namibia affair was a joke to George. He developed a theory that the graduate student had stolen the tape, claimed its contents as his own, and then sold the bootlegged music in Namibia. Useless for me to try to persuade him that the kind of music he wrote probably wasn't very popular in Namibia. "He's very subtle," said George gloomily of the putative thief. Some of the last letters he laboriously wrote, early in

2006, explained this conspiracy theory to friends, mostly old friends with whom George had been out of touch for years. "The thief has not been caught," he wrote in one letter. In another, though, he derived some comfort from the situation: "I console myself that imitation is the sincerest form of flattery." Many of these letters were sent to outdated addresses and were returned.

Maybe there was a grain of truth here too, in this mysterious pack that had "pitched" into him. But if such an elusive kernel existed, I couldn't find it. The world of the Namibia caper, or of this pack, wasn't a world I had the key to. I tried, half-heartedly, one last time.

"George? What pack?"

He shook his head. I think maybe he made an effort to shape his lips into a word: "No." Or maybe two words, such as "I can't." Anyway, no sound came out.

"It's okay, honey," I said. "It doesn't matter. Lunch will be ready soon."

He walked down the long hall and lay down to wait for lunch. At least that's how I conceptualized his waits as they punctuated his days. The truth is I don't know what he was waiting for or if he was waiting for anything at all.

CHAPTER 20

And I Awoke and Found Me Here

During that fall of 2007, I taught a course in Romantic poetry, and we spent the last few weeks of the course reading that quintessentially autumnal poet Keats, born on Halloween and author of "Ode to Autumn." Revisiting Keats's "La Belle Dame Sans Merci," the haunting ballad-like narrative that seems to say more to me each time I read it, reminded me of the traces Keats's poem had left on a little lyric of mine, "The Cold Hill Side."

In Keats's poem, the knight-at-arms (or wretched wight, depending on which version you're looking at) recounts the strange story of his abduction by the fairy figure of the title. His narrative climaxes with a nightmare vision from which he awakens. Abandoned, bewildered, telling his story to a questioner who seems well meaning but equally confused, the knight is the romantic equivalent of a survivor of alien abduction:

> And there she lulled me asleep,
>   And there I dreamed—Ah! woe betide!
> The latest dream I ever dreamed
>   On the cold hill's side.
>
> I saw pale kings and princes too,
>   Pale warriors, death-pale were they all;
> Who cried—"La belle Dame sans Merci
>   Hath thee in thrall!"

I saw their starved lips in the gloom
  With horrid warning gapèd wide,
And I awoke and found me here
  On the cold hill's side.

Though "The Cold Hill Side" was published in July 2007, I had started the poem years earlier, not long after the death of my friend Charles Barber in 1992. Thinking back to my short, joyful friendship with Charlie, who died of AIDS just after his thirty-fifth birthday, I have to acknowledge that my connection to him signaled even then some kind of failure of my conversation with George, some kind of loneliness—long before any cognitive problems surfaced—at the heart of our marriage. "The Cold Hill Side" can be read as an elegy, but it applies equally well to the uncanniness of the situation in which I found myself in 2007.

The Cold Hill Side

As months and years accumulate,
I miss you more and more.
Forgetting where I put the key,
I sometimes find a door,

And other times feel stunned and lost,
Though living in my own
Body and life, presumably,
Bewildered and alone

As the knight, kidnapped and released
To a dim world, who said,
And I awoke and found me here
On the cold hill side.

When this poem was published, some readers who knew my situation mapped their knowledge of George's illness onto the little lyric. Lured, perhaps, by the word "forgetting," which could be construed as a coded reference to George's condition, a few people asked me if I hadn't intended him to be the poem's speaker. No, I told these readers, it wouldn't occur to me to put words into this silent man's mouth, or at least that hadn't been my conscious intention. In poetry I could only speak for myself, though my own experience should have told me that good poetry always transcends its occasion.

To wake up disoriented, confused, palely loitering in a strange place . . . A bleak little memory surfaces here, from around 2000, years after I'd written the poem, and years before George's illness declared itself unmistakably. And yet, and yet . . . I remember saying to George one morning while we were still in bed, "I miss the old George" or "I want the old George back" or words to that effect. And his reply: "I do, too." He knew for a while that something or someone was gone—that George who, when we were first living together, woke up every morning with puns popping out of his mouth. That George was never coming back. Now, even the George who recognized his own transformation has pretty much disappeared.

It is so easy to feel, when we wake up in the morning, that any loss or change, any frightening deterioration, was just a bad dream. (Or we may dream that all is well and wake up to the bleak reality, as in Milton's sonnet "Methought I Saw My Late Espoused Saint.") Years before I had to learn to stomach the indigestible fact of George's condition, I'd written my little poem that links the stunned bewilderment of taking in a diminished reality to the haggard Knight's attempt to orient himself to the cold hill side of his new world.

Keats's "La Belle Dame Sans Merci" was not the only poem that reopened itself to me as a result of teaching the Romantics. An unexpected benefit of teaching Keats proved to be getting reacquainted with a poem by Milton. It is surely NO ACCIDENT (as James Merrill is fond of repeating in his Sandover trilogy) that a student reporting on Keats in my Romantics course should have chosen to juxtapose Keats's sonnet

"When I Have Fears" with Milton's sonnet "How Soon Hath Time." It had been years since I'd read or thought about the latter poem; but poems are remarkably adept at biding their time. Indeed, the sestet of Milton's sonnet treats precisely the matter of biding one's time—in a word, of patience.

> Yet be it less or more or soon or slow,
> It shall be still in strictest measure even
> To that same lot, however mean or high,
> Towards which Time leads me, and the will of Heaven.
> All is, if I have grace to use it so,
> As ever in my great Taskmaster's eye.

"It" refers both to the speaker's "inward ripeness," mentioned in the octave, and more generally to his destiny. Feeling he hasn't accomplished much by the age of twenty-three, he surrenders his future into the hands of his "great Taskmaster."

I happened to encounter this poem at a time in the fall of 2007 when I felt increasingly stymied precisely by the flow of time. It was a period when I was trying to decide not only what to do but how to feel, and how to respond, beyond futile flailing, to a disease whose course no human power could change. And here was Milton grappling with a challenge that, while certainly not identical, was in some ways similar. How to live in time? How to orient your life in relation to an uncontrollable and inscrutable future? Milton refers to "grace" and to his "great Taskmaster," two concepts one rarely comes across in the voluminous and ever burgeoning literature on dementia and caregiving. Furthermore, though I think I understand what Milton means by "grace," belief in a taskmaster isn't exactly available to me. Nevertheless, Milton's luminous sestet made me reflect that, hard though it continued to be, I was gradually learning to live with the "less or more or soon or slow" factor in a less, well, ungracious way than before. I had certainly had, and would continue to have, plenty of time to get used to this "lot."

Still, I couldn't help turning the situation over in my mind. Such a turning is in fact one way we get used to anything new, confusing, or intractable. When I considered George's condition, I kept rehashing it, reformulating it in my head or on paper or in histories to (how many?) doctors or well-meaning questioners. In so doing, I risked boring or alienating all my hearers (hapless wedding guests, maybe, whom I buttonholed as if I were the Ancient Mariner), with the possible exception of medical personnel. Telling versions of George's and my story over and over didn't make me feel any better. Constantly thinking or talking about his illness was an additional drain, a slow leak—wasn't living alongside it enough? But not talking or thinking about it were simply not options.

"I've gotta use words when I talk to you," says Sweeney in T. S. Eliot's *Fragment of an Agon*. In our household, though, the time had come when words as a way of communicating no longer worked nearly as well as food or the TV or the mercifully omnipresent cats. I no longer used language much, either to give George information which he would immediately forget or to tell him how I felt, which would upset me without making much of a dent in his carapace. It was also the case (is this the new Rachel speaking?) that when I was with George, I often didn't seem to feel much of anything. This flat new terrain seemed perfectly livable while I was in the middle of it. Anger, sadness, pity, boredom, frustration, desperation, exhaustion—even these eventually got flattened out.

Much has been written about dementia as an insidious disease. Few writers, however, talk about the insidiousness of the way a person living alongside the disease is first blind to it and then grows used to it. Three years after the diagnosis, and almost a decade, I would guess, after the first manifestations of the problem, I had gradually grown so accustomed to this impoverished and paralytic state of affairs that, alarming as it feels to say so, the situation did sometimes seem like the new normal. In time—less or more or soon or slow, but at some point—this new normal would cede to another, more diminished new normal. In fact, this process was happening already. And then, if I had grace to use it so, I would adjust. Or something would change.

CHAPTER 21

Failure Spreading Back up the Arm

"Proleptic," that's the word I want. Just to make sure, I'd better look it up in the *Oxford English Dictionary*, the two-volume boxed set that comes with its own magnifying glass in a little pull-out drawer. It's a Sunday morning, fall 2007. In the living room, George is trying to find Italian soccer or tennis on TV, but he keeps getting Nascar races instead. I walk away from the television, though not its noise, and over to the bookcase in the dining room. I think I know what proleptic means, but I need a definition. Here it is: "The representation or taking of something future as already done or existing; anticipation."

Anticipation means looking ahead to something, so that part of the definition doesn't quite seem to fit. I think of proleptic (and the first part of the definition backs me up) as a forward look tinged or undercut by blowback, so that the future to which one is looking ahead leaks back onto the present.

All day, no, all week, no, for the past two weeks, but with more concreteness of purpose and imagery each day, I have been thinking about what's euphemistically called "placement." This term refers to moving "a loved one" into an assisted living facility. There are other names for these places. Fighting my way through the circumlocutions that sprout around this subject like the thorn hedge in Sleeping Beauty, I've encountered, for example, on the lips of a doctor from Canada, the term "disposition," a euphemism for "placement," which is itself a euphemism.

Placement, disposition: whatever one calls it, many emotions arise even from the idea of this apparently unnamable deed. For placing a person means more than just moving him from home to Institution X. The placer first has to do the homework: check out the available options, make the financial arrangements, and last but not least, face the emotional jolts that accompany a foray (even a mental preview) into this territory, among them sadness and regret, guilt and relief, a sense of defeat and a sense of triumph. There are certainly many more feelings—irritation, for example, and tenderness; worry and boredom. This paired thinking reflects the obverse/reverse havoc the whole prospect wreaks on the placer.

At some point, all these emotions make sense—in retrospect if not in prospect—and it doesn't surprise me that they tend to arrive in contradictory dyads. What I haven't expected is for such jostling feelings, which refer at this point to something in the future, to be flowing so swiftly, so directly, back into the present. Yet this is exactly what they're doing. I envision institutionalizing George, and I immediately imagine feeling guilty or glad about it, and the guilt and gladness are right here with me, now, coursing invisibly through the dining room where I stand with the magnifying glass in my hand as I look up "proleptic."

And as these feelings seep backward from the anticipated future to the experienced present, this mild, autumnal Sunday unexpectedly takes on a tragic clarity and weight. Let's see if I can parse what's going through my head: I ought to be enjoying this time with my husband while we still live together, but knowledge of what is coming, or rather the imagination of what will, what might eventually be coming, makes enjoying the present almost impossible.

Maybe I should think of this intrusion of imagination as a way of prepaying my future debt of guilt. Maybe when the moment of placement actually arrives, I will have exhausted all my guilt—there'll be nothing more to pay. I don't actually believe this, though. Guilt seems an inexhaustibly self-renewing resource; there's always more where it came from.

Even assuming I could expunge the guilt and block thoughts of the future, it is still nearly impossible to enjoy the present with George. He is so barely present here and now that the ever-slender present grows even more exiguous; in fact, it vanishes from inanition. The vacuum where the present should be highlights what's left—the past and the future. Past: some good years with George, some not so good years; and for the past decade or so, the slow leakage of self I have lived alongside. Future: proleptic.

I put volume P–Z of the *OED* back in its case and the magnifying glass back in its drawer. I maneuver the heavy two-volume set back into its place on the lowest shelf of the bookcase; and I edge over in search of another book. I want a poem by Philip Larkin, but I'm not sure of its title, let alone which volume it's in.

Luck is with me. The first Larkin book I pull out is *The Whitsun Weddings*, and almost immediately I find the poem, though I'd been uncertain of almost every detail about it except the central image.

> *As Bad as a Mile*
> Watching the shied core
> Striking the basket, skidding across the floor,
> Shows less and less of luck, and more and more
>
> Of failure spreading back up the arm
> Earlier and earlier, the raised hand calm,
> The apple unbitten in the palm.

I've never seen (not that I ever looked for it) any suggestion that one of Larkin's signature subjects is dementia. Yet the desolation and loss, the sense of blank endings, of which

Larkin is surely one of the undisputed masters in twentieth-century poetry ("The Old Fools" and "Aubade" are two of the poems that showcase such themes, but there are many others, including the lapidary six lines of "As Bad as a Mile"), are disconcertingly appropriate to the precise range of issues that the thought of institutionalization brings up.

"Proleptic": the backward leaching of an imagined future. Here the future is failure. Larkin's little poem nails failure's retroactive dynamic. In "As Bad as a Mile," whose title wryly revises the familiar phrase (itself far from consoling), the failure is first of all—or is it last of all?—the thrower's failure to land the apple core in the basket.

The failure that haunts me today, that has been haunting me for weeks, involves my marriage of nearly thirty years. Much of the failure is mine. I am failing to imagine a future with him; failing to envision how I can summon the strength to go on like this; failing to remember him as he was before this illness stealthily took hold, to conjure him clearly enough so that some significant remnant of him is left to me. But there's plenty of failure to go around, and some of the failures are his: longstanding failures not only of memory and language but also of empathy and insight. As all these failures push me toward the null solution of "placement," even this present moment with him, this mild, slow Sunday, is being eaten away at by the anticipated future projecting itself proleptically back, with the majestic force ("the raised hand calm") of gravity.

Is Larkin's poem suggesting that the shied core's missing the wastebasket means that whatever the intention of the unlucky or unskilled thrower, the core was always doomed to miss? Or that the fact of the bad throw makes the core's missing the basket seem inevitable from the start? And if so, is this inevitability some sort of stoical or fatalistic consolation ("there never was a chance"), or does it make the misthrow even worse?

There are probably no answers to such questions. But when I did suddenly make up my mind, not to toss George into a basket but to "place" him, some of the responses I got seemed to touch upon a sense of inevitability. "Oh, I'm so glad you finally did it," one colleague said. "I wondered when you'd do this," said another. "It was never a matter of whether; it was a matter of when."

It strikes me now, trying to transcribe even a few comments, that each person succeeded unintentionally in conveying a small piece of what I was feeling. There was sadness, pity, relief, defeat, tenderness—the familiar gamut, except that guilt was reserved for me alone. Of course, no one person I spoke to expressed the intrinsic ambivalence, the warring impulses, the eagerness and dread and fatalism and determination that must somehow mix into a stable compound to enable the person responsible for taking this step to take it. No person could hold these strong feelings in suspension, give them a shape we can grasp, an articulation we can remember. No one person could. But sometimes poetry can.

CHAPTER 22

The Chorus

November 2007. For anyone old enough to remember the *Masterpiece Theatre* hit of the 1970s, here in the basement of the Metropolitan Museum there's a pervasive feeling of upstairs/downstairs. The three well-coifed young women with prettily draped scarves who work in the museum's Education Department seem to belong upstairs, while we, members of the caregivers support group that's meeting in the museum today, are downstairs. In fact, this division would be inaccurate: the Education Department is all located downstairs. It even has a separate portal (a tradesmen's entrance?), street-level, humble, inconspicuous, utterly different from the grand staircase up which the public proceeds to the museum's main doors.

The three young women have shepherded us into the large subterranean seminar room where we are now sitting. This is one of several support groups I've joined. Although their functions overlap, their intended targets aren't identical, and I haven't found them to be redundant. The people meeting here at the Met today are members of a group specifically for family members of people suffering from frontotemporal dementia. Another group I attend regularly meets under the auspices of Well Spouse, a wonderful national organization for the spouses and partners of people who are permanently ill or disabled. Later on I would help to organize yet another group, this one for spouses and partners of residents at the facility

George moved to. But that's getting ahead of myself. Support groups are crucial for someone in a situation like mine; there is no substitute for the kind of fellowship and comprehension one encounters there. Like the gifts of the imagination I mentioned earlier, such groups may not be sufficient—they can't solve the situation—but they are damned well necessary.

A conference room (like this one, windowless, but with an air of comfort) at the Alzheimer's Association in midtown is the usual venue for our bimonthly meetings. But today, thanks to an initiative intended to provide the dementia sufferers with cultural stimulation and their caregivers with respite, we're meeting underground in the Education Department of the Met. It seems to be a high-tech room, like a very smart classroom: adjustable lighting, screens on the walls for projections, who knows what other equipment. Only the too-small table we're grouped around fails to fit into the sleek surroundings; it looks like two tables from an elementary school classroom arranged to form one oblong. The surrounding space dwarfs the table, but we cluster around it anyway: the Three Graces, as I now find myself thinking of the museum staff members; Jane, the leader of our FTD support group; and the rest of us, mostly wives caring for their husbands.

What makes it so tempting to think of this scene as an upstairs/downstairs scenario is the pervasive sense of layering. There's the art layer of the museum (itself stratified) upstairs. Down here below street level, the educational missions of the museum are planned. Most of these efforts will ultimately involve exploration of the upper floors, the world where people float along, visit the gift shop, line up for blockbuster shows. Down here there's less floating and drifting and more talking and planning. For example, today's agenda calls for the young women to get a sense from us caregivers of what kind of art tour upstairs might work best for our loved ones.

And therein lies another kind of stratum, what one might call a cultural layer or a layer of discourse. The Three Graces who now crowd around the inadequate table with us have (I imagine) recently majored in art history, but they also clearly are interested in psychology or mental health, as well as, I'd assume, public relations and grant-writing. They look like Graces, but they talk like a cross between public relations personnel and social workers: an initiative here, a euphemism ("We don't use the word 'dementia'") there. This underworld seems like just the right place for euphemisms; the place *is* a sort of euphemism, come to think of it.

For it's not only spatially that we are below ground; not only architecturally that this is the lower level. As if the River Lethe instead of the traffic on Fifth Avenue were flowing past the museum, just outside its sturdy walls, we here in the windowless seminar room have crossed the stream of oblivion. Or rather we have sat in the boat escorting others—escorting, in the dialect of caregiving, our loved ones. The graceful nymphs who have ushered us into this underground chamber are free to get up and go. In fact, two of them soon do take their leave; the third remains, part observer, part perhaps custodian. But the rest of us are not really free to leave—not so long as the people who have drunk the waters of oblivion are in our keeping. We can and do put on our coats at the end of the session and find our way upstairs and out into the twilight. But in a way we remain in the subterranean dimness, paddling down Lethe along with our loved ones.

These people whose plight has brought us together here, for whom we are permanently responsible—where are they? They are not here, but we conjure them by talking about them. Talking about them is the purpose of our meetings. In today's unaccustomed venue, the Three Graces speak about the social and cultural benefits for the cognitively challenged of gallery visits while we caregivers get some down time, or possibly even get our own guided tour. We are grateful, but if I read the mood in the room right, we soon grow a little impatient with this kind of talk; we're ready for the nymphs to finish their presentation and return to the realm of daylight. We have other business down here—business that has nothing to do with looking at art.

Our loved ones aren't here. But we are gathered here because taking care of them is such a challenge, and because in the course of our caregiving we often understand one another better than anyone else understands us. All the recipients of our care suffer from one or another form of a brain malady that affects memory and judgment, language and behavior, personality and initiative. Some forms of this disease make them behave more like shades drifting through the nether world than like the bustlers up above. For all of them, the onset of the illness was gradual. At first nothing was detectable; then subtle signs appeared whose significance can only be read in retrospect. We caregivers, we observers, are the opposite of Orpheus in the underworld: we could only grasp a thing or a person by looking back over our shoulders. By the time we come to this room, the signs are clear, or clear enough—though in the misty realm of dementia, nothing is very clear. For some, both shades and caregivers, the sojourn in this realm ends abruptly with a death; for most of us, it stretches out in time and space.

So here we all are, daughters and wives, son and husband, assembled around an absence. If the three young women who led us down here are like helpful nymphs from Greek mythology, then we are a Greek Chorus. The heroes and heroines of our dramas are—as often happens in Greek tragedy—offstage; that is why we are free to ponder them. Wait, though—are we also messengers? True, we do tell stories to one another. But little of what we say is as definitive, let alone dramatic, as the report of someone's poking out his own eyes with the brooches of his dead wife's robes; or of a princess who puts on a poisoned dress and crown and melts before the horrified onlookers' eyes; or of a mad mother who tears off her son's head in the frenzied belief that he is a lion. Our tales are very tame by comparison. At most, as with the story of the man who mistakes his car for a golf cart, they provoke welcome chuckles. Choruses are not in the business of catharsis. Instead, we offer one another wisdom wrung from collective experience; hence the aphoristic tone of what we say.

When I first read Greek tragedy as a teenager, I was disappointed by what seemed (at least in my father's prose translation of Euripides) to be the abstract language of the Chorus at moments of crisis, dealing as it so often did in bland and obvious generalities while gruesome deeds were taking place offstage. Now all this makes much more sense. Ideal spectators, the Chorus has been called, helpless bystanders unable to affect the action. Yet Choruses certainly proffer advice. Sometimes, indeed, as if to insure that their words will not affect any outcomes, the Chorus are sworn to secrecy by one of the other characters in the drama—a feature neatly matched by the confidential nature of our support groups.

This afternoon, there's a newcomer in the group, Alice, whose daughter Joan, a woman in her forties, has come before. (To preserve confidentiality, I have changed names and stories.) Alice's husband and Joan's father is the man who drove his car onto the course at their Florida golf club. The conversation turns, as it has on other occasions, to the challenge of how to prevent people who should no longer drive from driving. "I can't just take his keys away," says Alice. "My mother is still in denial," says Joan gently. Mother and daughter, both lawyers, alert and watchful and sad, sitting side by side, appear to be very much in tune with each other. But Joan is scanning the terrain ahead with clearer eyes. She isn't the one who has to live with her father.

"It's hard enough that he's had to give up his medical practice," says Alice. "He wants to rent a new office. His profession was his whole identity. He keeps saying to me, 'If I'm not a doctor, who am I?' And then we get into terrible arguments.

Besides, a lot of the time he seems to be absolutely fine. Patients call him and want to set up appointments."

Sitting on my right, across the narrow table from Alice and Joan, is Steve, whose mother is bedridden and mute with Pick's disease, one of frontotemporal dementia's many manifestations. He listens to other people carefully, as in this room we all do; and when he speaks about other people's problems, he is usually right on target.

"Listen to me," he says urgently to Alice. "You need to change your perspective, to shift the way you are looking at this. A time will come when you'll be glad to have been able to have this much communication with him, even if it involved arguing. You will look back, believe me, and treasure these conversations as times when you still preserved some of the intimacy of a husband and wife."

And Alice listens in her turn, as intently as if he is giving her lifesaving instructions. The gravity and openness in the room, the spareness and unsentimentality—these, in this windowless room, are our source of light.

The last arrival, maybe half an hour into our conversation, is a pleasant-looking man I've never seen before. He's a little disheveled, hair rumpled and tie askew, as if he's been rushed or harried on his journey to the lower level. He sits down and Jane invites him to tell his story. There won't be time for everyone today, and newcomers trump veterans.

He doesn't waste words. It's his wife. They have eighteen-year-old twins, boy and girl, college freshmen. He agonizes over telling his children about their mother's recent diagnosis. How on earth will he manage to break this awful news to them?

"It may not be as hard as you think," various members of our Chorus tell him. "Very likely they already sense something." "It may even be a relief to them to hear the truth."

He has other challenges too. He worries—and this is a worry Alice has brought up earlier in today's session—about telling friends in his close-knit suburban community about his wife's illness. Who to tell first, and how to tell them? Come to think of it, why tell them yet? Why tell them at all?

This time the response comes from me. With complete assurance, a gift, I guess, of the past three years, I hear my voice saying, "If you don't tell people, then they cannot help you."

CHAPTER 23

Crusoe

It's the night after Christmas, 2007, cold and rainy. George is in bed by seven, as usual, and I walk down Broadway to Eighty-fourth Street to take myself to *The Water Horse*, a movie about the Loch Ness Monster. The shining water and the characters' freckled faces and fair skin; the fairy-tale quality of both setting and plot; the World War II time frame, so that the child hero's mother dresses rather as my mother-in-law did (and would indeed have been born at about the same time as my mother-in-law, whose maiden name was Ross, and who was proud of her Scottish descent)—all these features of the film unexpectedly and vividly bring back Squirrel Island.

On Squirrel Island, off Boothbay Harbor in Maine, my husband's parents and his paternal grandparents before them had a summer cottage, as these houses were called. George and I spent time on Squirrel Island in the summers of 1977 and 1978. Early in 1979, his mother, Connie, had a crippling stroke, and thenceforward could no longer go to the island, no longer welcome her children and daughters-in-law and grandchildren, no longer unite disparate temperaments, for short stretches at least, with her hospitality. Later, when our son was young, we returned to the island with him. Framed photos, now hanging in the bathroom of our New York apartment, verify that we were there for three summers in the late 1980s. Such photos, taken each summer at Squirrel, show all the children on the island, or all those who could be corralled onto the library steps for a group snapshot. There they stand or sit, some only toddlers, some almost teenagers: tanned, beaming, overwhelmingly blond.

The scenes in *The Water Horse* most evocative of Squirrel Island are set indoors, in the shed of the stately home where Angus, the film's young hero, hides the outsized egg he has found on the shore of the loch. The shed reminds me of the back porch of the cottage on Squirrel Island. This porch's sandy floor, swimming paraphernalia, set-tubs, washing machine and dryer, wonderful old foghorn, and much else I've forgotten, suggested both recreation and tradition, summer vacations and chores. Its various nooks and crannies were good places to stash especially beautiful stones or shells found on the beach.

My chronology gets foggy here, but the time came when George's brother and sister, both of whom had become full-time residents of the Boothbay area in the 1980s, saw no point in maintaining an expensive house on an exclusive island. George wasn't happy with their decision, but he certainly wasn't willing, even if he'd been able, to buy out his siblings' shares; besides, we had Vermont for summers. I shared his conclusion, though I too felt wistful at the loss of an irreplaceable house.

So we stopped going to the island that had been like a blue patch set in the middle of our green summers. Though vivid, it was always a small patch; we never spent more than ten days on Squirrel in any given summer. Gradually, inevitably, George's memories of the island recalled the happiest times of his childhood; of his mother's years of health and hospitality, gardening and cooking, arranging arduous lobster picnics on the rocks; and further back, of his father, who had died in 1961. George's father had spent happy adolescent summers boating around Squirrel in the 1910s. An eloquent snapshot depicts George's tall, black-clad, formidable grandmother showing a cowed-looking daughter-in-law around the garden.

A head shorter than her mother-in-law and by all accounts much milder, Connie didn't start to enjoy the cottage until the older generation had passed on.

The Squirrel Island cottage was sold in 1993. Connie's last nine or ten years were spent in a nursing home in Boothbay Harbor, where we used to visit her occasionally. If you craned your neck, you could catch a glimpse of ocean from the window of her room. The last time we saw Connie, she was no longer speaking, though she still smiled broadly when others spoke to her. Ever since her stroke she had spoken less and less. Until her death in 2001, she spent twenty-two years sitting in a chair, silent, waiting.

Christmas this year fell on a Tuesday. Today is Wednesday. Next Thursday, January 3, the plan is for me, our son Jonathan, my friend Lorna (to drive) and another friend, Serinity (for moral support), to take George up to White Plains and install him in an Alzheimer's facility. The tears that spring to my eyes at the end of *The Water Horse*—no, long before the end—they are for poor George, pacing silent and spectral and unsuspecting through the apartment, through the fall, through the holidays. They are for me, bearing the weight of this knowledge, not to mention the weight of the past few years. Like a load on my head, I carry the fact of this looming change, as in the film Angus's mother carries, unbeknownst to her young son, the weight of the knowledge that she is a widow and her children are fatherless, that their father drowned when the Nazis sank his ship. They are tears of guilt and knowledge, and tears of pity: pity for George, pity for me. Tears for the long decline, for the many years that my husband, our boy's father, was gradually fading, being leached away so slowly that none of us understood until quite late in the process—not that understanding earlier would have made much difference. Tears for our son Jonathan, who was effectively fatherless from the age of thirteen or so. During our long talk this Christmas Eve, Jon told me that he'd never had an adult conversation with his father.

Back, back, back. I want to leap much further back, back to a time not only before this long decline started but back to a boyish George I never knew but can easily imagine, playing tennis on the clay courts on Squirrel Island, splashing at the Hotel Beach, or pumping water, after a hurricane damaged the island's pipeline, at the Cove Beach; back to a later George composing music on the glassed-in porch of the cottage, using the rickety old upright piano his father had reportedly fished out of the sea at low tide—or was it out of the island dump? This piano stood in a tiny room off the dining room, so when George was working, he used to stride back and forth the length of the rooms between his piano and his desk.

Of this youthful George, a person I've heard about and seen in photographs, and whom I knew during our brief times on Squirrel, especially before Connie's stroke, I find myself the repository, the custodian, just as I seem to have undertaken the role of custodian of his books and papers, his scores and sketches, his essays. His siblings, his colleagues, his friends, even his son: none of them can penetrate his thick isolation. In truth, no one has been able to get through it for years, including me. But I've undoubtedly been the closest to this walled-in person, and I am the one with whom people leave messages.

In a roundabout way, the light-hearted holiday movie has helped me carry my burden for one rainy night, at the beginning of the awful countdown toward "placement." It has helped by reminding me that there were other times and places in George's life, that things weren't always like this. *The Water Horse* reminded me, too, that I'd spent time on that magical island which I hadn't thought of in years. I had taken my toddler down to a beach teeming with blond, freckled youngsters, and he splashed and played, or we built sandcastles. If we never saw a benign monster, such as *The Water Horse* depicts, sail serenely out to sea, maybe it was because we failed to look up at the right moment.

Silent in his chair or on the sofa, or lying on the bed waiting for the next meal, George has become a sort of monster himself—not evil and frightening, nor playful and exuberant like the aquatic creature of *The Water Horse*, but awe-inspiring, off-putting, uncanny. Sherry Turkle notes in *Evocative Objects* that Freud said "we experience as uncanny those things that are 'known of old yet unfamiliar.'" The uncanny, Turkle continues, "is not what is most frightening and strange. It is what is seen close but 'off,' distorted enough to be creepy. It marks a complex boundary that both draws us in and repels."

The fatherless boy Angus serves as father surrogate to the helpless, hungry, floundering young monster, which, inspired by his reading, he names Crusoe. For these past few years, certainly since his diagnosis early in 2005, George has lived in a Robinson Crusoe-like isolation. But the condition of isolation goes much, much farther back. How far? Where does personality shade into pathology? Pondering just this painful and unanswerable question in *The Story of My Father*, Sue Miller posits that "it seems possible . . . that Alzheimer's is a lifelong disease whose expression in dementia is simply the closing episode, a kind of crossing the threshold for the long-failing brain, the last step that finally makes clear what earlier steps have meant." Miller writes, too, of "wondering whether some aspects of [her father's] personality that seemed so essentially who he was might really have been the disease expressing itself."

George's personality, and then his disease, increasingly expressed itself through silence. If there was one reason I decided that I could no longer live with George, that coordinating his care had gone from arduous and unrewarding routine to unbearable pain, that reason was the grinding loneliness imposed by his silence, the almost unbroken silence, as it now seems to me, of an insidious but remorseless—what noun do I need here? Do I mean enemy, or person, or illness? Or perhaps what Carolyn Feigelson, writing of her husband's traumatic brain injury, in her article "Personality Death, Object

Loss, and the Uncanny," has called the doppelganger at the dinner table?

The apartment has been silent during the days while the holidays went by outside, silent after George went to bed at six or seven on the dark December evenings. As the days have shortened and the little natural light we might get through our north-facing living room window has been blocked off by a greenish-black veil put up by construction workers, I may have been confusing and conflating the darkness with the silence. But my intuitions aren't confused; they feel pure, distilled, clear. I know what I can no longer bear and what I must do.

And knowing this hurts doubly. First is the knowledge of what I'm feeling, and of where this comes from. As each layer of realization gives way to an earlier, underlying layer, the dull scab of dailiness breaks and the wound bleeds. Second is the necessary concealment of this knowledge, of my own pain. As soon as I decided that this placement would have to happen and happen soon; as soon as I'd made the necessary arrangements and the countdown began, I immediately had to begin carrying the decision, shielding George from knowledge both of the place I'd reached and how I'd gotten there.

Back and forth the pendulum had swung. When our interests and needs no longer coincided, what was the best thing for both of us? For him? For me? For our son? When George no longer taught, composed, played the piano, read, wrote? When he had almost completely ceased smiling, speaking? When he was sleeping fourteen hours a day? This long-suspended question did abruptly answer itself with a clarity for which I was and am grateful. But the answer was painful nonetheless.

Now zero hour is looming. I have been advised not to tell George, won't tell him, can't tell him we are going anywhere until the morning of the day we go. How we'll get him into my friend's car, and then out of it in White Plains, are questions I haven't answered yet. The necessity of figuring out such answers by myself underscores how lonely the past ten years have been.

Suddenly, sharply, another feeling cuts into the mix: the prospect of his leaving stabs me with remorse. And I find I'm abruptly remembering what it felt like, a long time ago, to love him. The Loch Ness creature of *The Water Horse*, with its exuberant splashing, diving, flipping, and somersaulting for the sheer fun of it, reminds me what that delight feels like. This kind of physical energy, the joy of being alive expressed as movement, which no one in my family has ever had much of, George used to have in spades—energy to burn. He still retains faint—sometimes not so faint—traces of it. This energy, like so much else about him, has now been committed to my weary, overburdened keeping.

CHAPTER 24

The Poet and the Drudge

Here's a pseudo-Zen koan I came up with, which I used to intone in various support group meetings: "Habituation is the enemy of resolution." Yet despite the blandishments offered by habituation—its comforts, its snug inertia—I did eventually resolve that our apartment was no longer the best place for George. Or maybe I should say I resolved that to have George at home was no longer the best thing for me or him.

Sometime between Thanksgiving and Christmas 2007, my mind made itself up. When it came, the decision seemed to some people—even in a way to me—sudden, abrupt. Other people—Jane, who ran the FTD support group; Heleena, the social worker in the neurologist's practice—commented that I had been talking about placing George for a year or more. My nephew Edward wrote me that I was like a beginning swimmer nervously circling the deck of the pool, always saying I'd go in "next year," then suddenly taking a deep breath and just jumping.

For a long time I had been plodding along, putting one foot in front of the other. I'd been doing some research with the help of a website called APlaceforMom.com. Early in November 2007 I visited a homey assisted-living facility in a mansion in Montclair, New Jersey. Back in the spring of that year, I'd visited two places in Manhattan and one in Westchester County. But the double track prevailed: I trudged through my daily life, went to school and taught and came home. I talked about placing George. I thought about it. But I also *didn't* think about it. The whole concept seemed unattainably distant and unreal.

In retrospect, I can see that I was approaching some kind of limit. No doctor or other professional said, "It's time"— or rather, the only doctor to have said anything like this had written it to me back in January 2007, after we visited him in Philadelphia. Nothing in George's condition had dramatically worsened. Some of the people I'd got to know in support groups had been advised by doctors or family members that it was no longer possible to care for the sick person at home. Sometimes things became very clear: there was a threat, or more than a threat, of violence. Sometimes the illness took a drastic turn. But I was never afforded that clarity.

I know that a death affected me. Veronica, a reference librarian at Rutgers-Newark, diagnosed with cancer in May, died in early December 2007 at about the age of fifty. I was one of many Rutgers colleagues who was asked to speak at her memorial service. I remember that I read George Herbert's poem "Virtue." (Herbert was always a favorite of George's, who had set some of his poems for soprano and piano.) "Sweet day, so cool, so calm, so bright": Veronica seemed to me to have had a cool, calm brightness, coupled with warmth, curiosity, a gift for friendship, and a zest for a number of activities including her work as a librarian but also swimming, traveling, antiquing. It was a life that was cut off, but it was a full life. Her husband, her large family in Canada, her many Rutgers colleagues in and out of the library—all of them would now have to deal with her absence. But the memories were fresh and vivid and positive; almost until the very end, Veronica had been alert and aware, sharp and funny. All these qualities had been taken away, still were being taken away, from George, piece by slow piece.

After the service for Veronica, I returned to the city and met my friend Dawn for a late dinner. An aide was making

George's dinner; by that time, I was in the habit of making sure I arrived home after he was in bed. The restaurant was loud and crowded, but over the clashing of dishes and the buzz of other conversations, Dawn and I managed to talk. I was sad and tired; she was feeling overwhelmed by the needs of her demented mother, recently widowed, and even more by the demands of her husband's stepmother, also recently widowed. She didn't live with these people, so the burden was more removed. But she felt bowed down by obligations and guilt, feelings which would probably last as long as these women lived. Then again, these women were old: the mother in her eighties, the stepmother in her nineties. George was just sixty-four.

I lay awake that night, and for reasons I do not know, but which felt then and still feel now connected with that memorial service and that dinner, I crossed a line in my mind. This life I was living was too hard, and it could easily go on, getting gradually harder, for decades. I was exhausted and lonely. George was less and less present.

Was this the right thing to do and the right time to do it? Not counting George, the only person besides me whose life would be affected by my decision was our son. Jon had been saying for months that I best understood the burden I was carrying and should do what I had to do. And my sister and my nephew, who both offered understanding and moral support, knew that it was my decision.

As it happened—and I suspect the sequence often unfolds more or less this way—once I made up my mind, the window of opportunity for getting George into a specific place was quite a narrow one. One of the facilities I'd visited the previous spring, Hearthstone in White Plains, had a bed. (The Manhattan Hearthstone had a long waiting list; and the other Manhattan facility I'd visited that spring, the Eightieth Street Residence, had struck me at the time as too chic, too Upper East Side.) The young director at White Plains was easy to talk to. We arranged that she and one of their nurses would come to the apartment a little before Christmas to do an assessment. They specified that the actual move would have to be on a weekday. From my point of view, it also had to be when Jonathan was in town, so he would be able to help. Jon's scheduled winter break—he was living in Albuquerque that year, studying Ayurveda—was complicated. And I already had plane tickets to visit my sister and Jon in Albuquerque in early January. All these considerations made it easy to fix on January 3rd as Placement Day. I implored the social worker, the doctor, the Alzheimer's Association, whoever would listen, for suggestions to help me manage the move, especially what to tell George. No one was particularly helpful, and I dealt with that problem by not dealing with it. The day worked out more or less as planned. It wasn't easy, but the mission was accomplished. I write this not to relive that difficult morning, which remains vivid in my memory, but rather to think about how making the decision felt.

In deciding to move George and then doing so as soon as was feasible—a matter of a few weeks—I broke through encrusted habit and entered a bald new territory. What had I imagined? If a diagnosis of dementia ushers one into a confusing world, then the day of placement or its aftermath ought to be the door out of that world. To an insidiously creeping process, this day applies a short sharp shock, a disjunction that demarcates more than one life into Before and After. Accordingly, I'd assumed that, however fraught the process, once it was over the outlines of my world—the post-placement world—would have a certain chilly clarity.

Clarity, though, eluded me. Yes, in the weeks leading up to the placement I had used my head, done some dogged factfinding about what was available, visited a few institutions, and engaged in a good deal of consultation with a sympathetic social worker and a responsive neurologist. But the imaginative labor, the emotional work involved in placing a loved one—

these assignments begin only as the factual part of the home-work ends. Nor do such tasks end naturally or obviously. I'm not sure they ever really end. At best, they taper off as inconspicuously as the disease began.

At the time I placed George, this imaginative work was work that I hadn't even started. Partly I hadn't known how to begin. Partly, too, I sensed that other kinds of work took precedence; that now, before George's move, was the time for what has been called the chopping wood and carrying water side of life. I did dimly sense that somewhere on the far side of the Before and After divide, such work would be awaiting me. I reckoned that I had the rest of our lives, George's and mine, to learn how this new state of affairs would feel—to familiarize myself with the place, the people, the process and protocols of visiting, not to mention the emotional ups and downs of it all. If this learning curve took time, time was one resource we had plenty of. I remember thinking, in a tiny burst of clarity in the first weeks after George moved out, that habit alone had enabled me to live with him for the past few years, and habit would also enable me to live without him.

When I thought ahead to life after George's move, I could only envision that cool new landscape: clean, uncluttered, simplified, maybe a bit bare—as if life at home with George hadn't also come to feel unendurably chilly and bare.

Yet how uncluttered and clear could this new terrain really be? Consider for starters the unpalatable glut of euphemisms (*loved one, placement, facility*) that becomes one's daily fare when one is in my situation. Euphemisms are enemies of clarity, and yet at times one must accede to them, because synonyms are either lacking, too cumbersome, or too painful. "Place" as a verb acquires a specialized meaning, as do the nouns "placement" and "facility" and "loved one." And to think that near the beginning of this struggle, back in 2004, I had resisted the word "caregiver" as too impersonal or institutional or just smarmy!

One does, however, have a choice. George Orwell put it this way in his essay "Politics and the English Language," a piece whose characteristic clarity casts a pitiless light on the word "placement" and its ilk:

> . . . if thought corrupts language, language can also corrupt thought . . . [The] debased language . . . is in some ways very convenient . . . When you think of something abstract you are more inclined to use words from the start, and unless you make a conscious effort to prevent it, the existing dialect will come rushing in and do the job for you, at the expense of blurring or even changing your meaning.

Blurring is the intention—perhaps a benign intention—of labels like "Life Guidance," a phrase that is sometimes used to refer to the dementia wing of an assisted-living facility. "Placement" itself is an apparently neutral term designed to convey, without undue vividness or specificity, a long drawn-out, costly, emotionally draining, and inevitably individual process. The use of ready-made labels seems to open the door for "the existing dialect [to] come rushing in and do the job for you."

I can't allow that to happen. Though I'm burdened with responsibilities and decisions I never expected to have to take on, I will not yield control of one of my remaining resources, the choice of words, which also happens to be one of my specialties. I use the word "placement" sometimes, as a lazy shorthand, but I also try to keep other words, and other thoughts, burnished, sharp, and ready for deployment.

But the murk of institutionalizing one's husband (let me not, for once, write "placing a loved one") only begins with nomenclature. The fog thickens as one advances. The ghostly forms swirling around in the gloom include, to name only a few, ambivalence, regret, guilt, sadness, and relief, interspersed in small bursts with the fierce glee of the survivor, the agent: "I did it! I got out alive!"

The bad news of diagnosis shuts off some choices and creates others. I didn't choose for George to become sick—no one did. But the step to move him out of our apartment was one someone had to make. In our little family, I was the one who had to make it. Sherwin Nuland encapsulates this dilemma in the Alzheimer's chapter of his book *How We Die*: "The difficulty of deciding is compounded by the difficulty of living with what has been decided." In other words, when it comes to scooping someone out of the house where they have lived for thirty years and inserting them into what the young writer Stefan Merrill Block calls, in his novel *The Story of Forgetting*, "The Waiting Room"—when it comes to doing this, there are no good choices.

It is not surprising that the large and expanding literature of caregiving is not the best place to learn this salient truth— a truth whose discomfort for all concerned is of large, almost unmanageable, proportions. In this context, myth helps more than euphemism: you try to steer past Scylla and Charybdis, but then you have to choose between the two.

Making a decision when, no matter what you choose, circumstances will press hard and painfully is a theme more sharply limned in tragedy than in the literature of caregiving. Richard Goodkin, a scholar of Euripides and Racine, describes what he beautifully and simply calls the tragic middle: "Tragedy tells us, as no other genre does, that even though not everything depends on us, even though we are acted on and constrained by forces beyond our control, nonetheless we must make unmakable choices." And further: "The tragic middle recognizes not only that, as has been said of the tragic hero, you can't have it both ways, but also that you must have it both ways."

You must have it both ways. The track remains stubbornly, unregenerately double. Before George left home—before, to mince no words, I moved him out—I could work, but with the shadowy weight of his spectral presence on my mind, in my heart. Now I can work more easily in many ways, but with the shadowy weight of his spectral absence, and my undeniable responsibility for, ownership of, that absence, on my mind, in my heart.

Yet the work goes on. I've already referred to the notion of the double track. In his novel *A Modern Instance*, William Dean Howells uses the phrase "dual life." Probably because I'm a writer, I found the following passage uncomfortably apt. A journalist's marriage is crumbling, his life is in crisis yet,

> at the same time he wrote more than ever in the paper, and he discovered in himself that dual life of which every one who sins or sorrows is sooner or later aware: that strange separation of the intellectual activity from the suffering of the soul, by which the mind toils on in a sort of ironical indifference to the pangs that wring the heart; the realization that in some ways his brain can get on perfectly well without his conscience.

I don't want to claim, nor do I think Howells is claiming, that writers are more heartless than other people. But that "ironical indifference to the pangs that wring the heart" precisely captures the detachment that necessarily attends the minutiae of institutionalizing someone. In fact, the detachment branches into two parts. First, there's the cool head required to organize financial and logistical matters. When I sent two boxes of George's clothing and toiletries by UPS to White Plains in case too much luggage in the car might make him suspicious, I ignored my inner turmoil. And second, there is that portion of one's consciousness that operates not only (as the cool head does) at a remove from but also (and here's the difference from the cool head) in emotional or intellectual response to, in acknowledgment of, the pangs of the imminent crisis, whether that crisis is external and public (a war, a hurricane) or domestic and private (illness, "placement").

In Cavafy's poem "Darius," the poet Phernazis is hard at work on an epic poem about King Darius when he is interrupted by the news that war with the Romans has begun.

Distracted and terrified, Phernazis nevertheless can't stop thinking about his poem in progress, whose theme ominously echoes or presages or recapitulates the situation he is facing. "But through all his distress, all the turmoil / the poetic idea comes and goes insistently . . ." Just so: through all the dull and wrenching process of decision-making and placement, through all the turmoil and distress, my poetic ideas too came and went insistently.

Call the fact-finding, facility-visiting drudge who was busy throughout the months before she institutionalized her husband D. Call the poet who cohabited with D in the same body and brain P. Scuttling through her days, D couldn't see the forest for the trees, and didn't want to. She carried a notebook and wrote down facts and figures she promptly forgot. She consulted websites and experienced confusion when, in response to information she'd typed in, two different employees, both named Holly, both with soothing voices, called her back. D never spelled out to herself where all her research about institutions was heading; she kept her nose to the grindstone and squirreled away data. (D's lazy fondness for clichés—dead metaphors, as Orwell points out, do our thinking for us—is no accident.)

Like D, P never said to herself in so many words that sooner or later she was going to move her husband out of the apartment. Unlike D, she knew subliminally that this would happen and kept wondering how it would feel. She dreamed about the transition; even in her sleep, she tried to picture the change. Above all, unlike D, who stuck strictly to prose, P wrote poems recording her dreams and imaginings before they evaporated under the daily glare of facts, the endless list of chores.

Sometimes P's poems, as poems do, used tropes to express what couldn't be said easily. Tropes are the opposite of pre-fab, one-size-fits-all euphemisms like "facility"; rather than blurring meaning, they create pictures in the mind. For example, in July 2007—six months before George was moved, and before D had any conscious intention of moving him—P wrote a poem that was her sole experiment in the blues form. The poem, whose original title was "Dementia Blues," tries to draw a picture of the illness by comparing it to the kind of place P didn't even consciously know George was headed. But such prophetic moments happened to P, or to her poetry, all the time.

Hotel

Living with dementia is like riding on a carousel.
I said dementia is a big old carousel.
And you can't get off, but it turns into a hotel.

Year after year they reserve you the same space.
Year after year they save you the same old place.
They forget your name, but they never forget a face.

Who's going to visit you? Don't expect your friends.
No use getting up for visits from your friends.
It goes on this way and who knows how it ends?

Well, you sit there, baby, and you don't say a word.
Yup, there you sit, not saying a single word.
Or if you did, I guess I never heard.

Sometimes I wonder what's going through your head.
Yes, who knows what is cooking in your head?
No one gets to look in there till you are dead.

I'd like to cry, but I have no more tears.
I said I'm done crying, I've run out of tears.
Before and now and after, years and years.

Another poem P wrote sometime during the year before George's move recorded and tossed around a seven-word sentence that had come to her in a dream. Weaving this sentence—"The future needs a place to stand"—into a villanelle didn't make it any less hermetic, but perhaps helped P to understand how challenging it would be to envision the future.

Can time be thought of as a place? P, who unlike D tended to jot down striking passages she came across in her reading, was interested to learn that attempting to conceptualize time as space was a well-worn trope. She read in Steven Pinker's *The Stuff of Thought*:

> In the *Time Orientation* metaphor, an observer is located at the present, with the past behind him and the future in front, as in *That's all behind us, We're looking ahead,* and *She has a great future in front of her.* . . . In the *Moving Time* metaphor, time is a parade that sweeps past a stationary observer: *The time will come when typewriters are obsolete; The time for action has arrived; The deadline is approaching; The summer is flying by.* But we also find a *Moving Observer* metaphor, in which the landscape of time is stationary and the observer proceeds through it: *There's trouble down the road; We're coming up on Christmas; She left at nine o'clock; We passed the deadline; We're halfway through the semester.*

In "Dream Sentences," the villanelle based on her seven-word sentence, P was less a moving observer proceeding through the stationary landscape of the future than she was a surveyor of that landscape preparatory to venturing into it, trying to find a foothold.

Dream Sentences

The future needs a place to stand.
But it's too cold for questions like these.
Take my hand.

Hope cannot be conjured at command.
I have a history of highs and lows.
The future needs a place to stand.

What others think be damned.
What I am living next to no one knows.
Let go my hand

and leave me solitary in the land
I live in, to confront its rains and snows.
The future needs a place to stand.

Some days I manage better than I planned;
the struggle doesn't show. Or else it shows.
Take my hand,

steady me, and let me sense the bond.
Well, sick, dead, or living: win or lose
the future. Let me have a place to stand.
Here is my hand.

P was also fascinated to read William James's account of the way in which, when we think of time as place, we look into time "in two directions":

> . . . the practically cognized present is no knife-edge, but a saddle-back, with a certain breadth of its own on which we sit perched, and from which we look in two directions into time. The unit of composition of our perception of time is a duration, with a bow and a stem, as it were—a rearward—and a forward-looking end . . . We do not first feel one end and then feel the other after it, and from the perception of the succession infer an interval of time between, but we seem to feel the interval of time as a whole, with its two ends embedded in it.

Moving into the post-placement future, P found herself the observer preparing to proceed into this new zone. But the time behind her, the time before placement, was still recent enough to be very vivid, very close.

In a poem written during a visit to New Mexico a week after George's move, P used the landscape—the foothills of the Sandia Mountains—as a literal place to stand while looking down into the valley of—of what? The past? The future? Or maybe just a valley? The past leading to this present she thought of as a road. This road continued on toward the future.

But where it had previously been as precarious as a tightrope, it was now just an ordinary road; one could walk on the ground. And yet the figure of the road is tentative; it ends with a question mark.

New Year

Blue January light, cold, scoured, clear.
From the Sandia foothills looking down
and back to where I came from, and the town
spread out below, then back to the past year,

or three or more years carrying this load,
how do I feel unburdened: free and light?
Unanchored, dizzy, my precarious tightrope lowered to a mere terrestrial road?

The blank new month requires divination.
Sword, wand, ship, sandal: at the Flying Star
(we talk our way along; improvisation),
the cards laid out spell struggle, choice, and pain;
also a white horse champing in a green
meadow; a maiden moving down a long dark stair.

Questions in poems are not always rhetorical. "How do I feel unburdened?" Well, how did P—how did I—feel? The trope of the road answered me. When one has little idea of what to expect, images serve better than words. The rest of the poem refers to a lunch at a local restaurant, poetically named the Flying Star (in fact there's a chain, or constellation, of these places), where my sister and two of her friends invited me to join them in laying out Tarot cards for the new year 2008. At once archetypal and ambiguous, images such as the Tarot offers are suggestive, versatile, applicable to all sorts of situations. Like dreams, these images may seem to depict either the past or the future, or both. But no matter how fluid their answers, how Delphic their responses, Tarot images (like any other form of divination) do not hand the diviner a list of euphemisms. The images provide the blank future with "a local habitation and a name." Or rather, we read the images and supply the local habitation and the name.

The sense of lived time as space turns up once more, in a poem I wrote the following month. (Wait. *I* wrote: so had D and P merged? The larger divide now was, maybe, between Before and After.) Six weeks after institutionalizing George, I (not surprisingly) came down with the flu. True, the flu vaccine that year had reportedly been less than effective; but in any case, hadn't I been storing up stress for months and years? Lying flat in bed for a couple of days wasn't a hard decision; I acceded gratefully to the necessity. Horizontal, gently suspended between past and future, sleeping a lot, I remembered more of my dreams than usual. And for a change, one of them harked back to a happy moment with George many years before.

"February Flu" begins by recalling several ominous dreams from the past year or so—dreams of being submerged, overwhelmed, drowned: easy-to-read dreams about going under. When the flu took over, I dreamed of intimacy, giggling, glee, sex—about youth.

All these dreams, both of dread and joy, referred to the past; they comprise the first stanza of "February Flu." But that past itself had now come to seem dreamlike. Even though the years George and I had spent together from our meeting in 1976 to the start of his illness some twenty years later outnumbered the years of the illness itself by two to one, it didn't feel that way. Instead, the happy past seemed as remote as a fairy tale, while the creeping disease and the hard years it ushered in shone with unwanted clarity.

There was still the future. In my woozy, feverish state, as I gazed sleepily at the snow falling outside the bedroom window, it was time to escape the before and after divide, the illness, the placement. I was so tired of being efficient, executive, decisive—of being, not only Drudge D, but an "I" at all. It was time to lie back and let feeling wash over me.

February Flu

The dreams of dread were dreams about the future.
We walked along the rocks at Squirrel; the tide
rolled in too high and fast. Or grey-green waters
rose past the rolled-up windows of a car
there was no getting out of—either way,
drowning the sole escape. This morning early,
a country house instead. An upstairs room
at dawn. We woke and turned to one another,
the summer day, the summer all before us,
and then before we touched I scrambled out
naked to shut the door which had been left
ajar. So, giggling, back to bed. The past.

Numerically those years outweighed the blank
of roads without a map, of rising water.
But both those landscapes now
have been relegated to the realm of dreams
and woken from are weightless, insubstantial.
Still slightly woozy from the flu, I lie
and watch late winter's white sift past the window.
Poised between glad memory and dread—
both now erased—I'm venturing step by step
into a solitary trackless country
that has yet to yield its secrets up.

A few people had ventured to predict how I would feel after George left. "You'll feel exhilarated, then guilty," said some. "You'll feel guilty, then exhilarated," said others. No one had said: "You'll lie flat, dreamy, exhausted."

CHAPTER 25

Your History Stacked Up

The sense of what a bare, fresh newness feels like is not only fleeting, it's hard to recapture. As the new and strange becomes the accustomed, habit clouds our memories. What Iris Origo, in her memoir *Images and Shadows*, calls the dust of daily life soon interferes with our ability to pay attention:

> After a place has become one's home, one's freshness of vision becomes dimmed; the dust of daily life, of plans and complications and disappointments, slowly and inexorably clogs the wheels.

The place that was my physical home was the same place George and I had moved into on a thundery afternoon in May 1978. I wasn't having to adjust to a new dwelling. And yet I was slowly reclaiming the space: it was becoming my home in a new and different way. Taking stock as winter turned into spring in 2008, I realized that I now had a new responsibility: I'd become an archivist.

Feeling like a repository wasn't a brand new experience. For years I'd been carrying around, somehow finding mental space for, George-related information to which George himself no longer had access. But this was different. George wasn't much of a packrat, but in his little study I found a disorderly mix of journals from his years at the American Academy in

Rome and letters from friends, mixed in with scores, syllabi, course notes, and yellowing clippings of reviews, all piled up higgledy-piggledy.

I employed Serinity to catalogue George's books, scores, and CDs. A few of the books and scores went to the Columbia music library; the bulk went to Rutgers. Some of the CDs of twentieth-century music I gave to acquaintances from the music world; the rest of the CDs I am still sifting, playing a few favorites, trying some new ones, and taking some with me whenever I go to visit George. If we listen to a familiar piece, he sometimes hums, a pleasing, barely audible sound deep in his throat. Occasionally he holds up a finger or makes a conducting gesture.

The reviews, program notes, miscellaneous professional and private correspondence, and sketches of pieces all went to Columbia. What remained had an orphaned, rootless air. The more recent a document, the more random and misplaced it was likely to be. From early 2006, I found several jiffy bags, some of which had contained CDs, addressed but never sent, or misaddressed and returned. The addresses were out of date in part because the people George was writing to came from prior layers in his life: Oberlin in the Sixties, the American Academy in Rome in the Seventies, MacDowell in the Eighties. This spate of mailings followed in the wake of George's retirement concert in December 2005 (a concert, as I've said, unfortunately marked by the failure of the person in charge to record it). After this fiasco, George wrote letters to several old friends, letters which reflected his preoccupation with this mishap.

Old postcards and Christmas cards also turned up in the mix of papers I was beginning gingerly to go through; anonymous snapshots of a wedding or a baby. There were quite a few valedictory paper placemats from George's various stays at MacDowell or the Virginia Center. The practice at such places is for the departing colonist to collect at that evening's dinner everyone's name and address and phone number (now it would include email and website) on his or her paper placemat.

One of the poems I wrote soon after George moved out evokes my looming archival chores. The responsibility seemed the greater, and the task the sadder, because there was no one to share it with. In the last few years, George had vanished from other people's lives. There would be his book of essays; there was a CD forthcoming. There were the beautiful hand-copied scores. But his audience, his circle of friends, his colleagues, his students: who and where were they? With a scant handful of exceptions, these groups of people had melted away.

The Stack

As if it weren't sufficient keeping track
of my own growing and unruly stack
of stuff going how many decades back,

here now are yours, piled in no special order.
"March 5. Snow. An hour before supper"
is how you'd date an average MacDowell letter.

Your archive is no more of a mess
than many people's—maybe a bit less.
Since I've known you, spareness, if not neatness,

as theme recurred. But loose now, anchorless,
your papers drift: an empty CD case,
a letter lost with no return address.

If you die first, a few old students may
recount their distant memories of you
to me. If you survive me, possibly

to our son. Frantic Andromache
tells Hector: "You are all in all to me.
You and my son are our whole family."

Not that the situations are the same.
Still, we are all the family you can claim,
I and our son outside your silent room,

your history stacked up inside my brain.

It took a year to do it, but eventually I did begin unpacking and unstacking the most personal part of George's archive—his letters to me. Looking at old letters from anyone you've loved isn't easy, whether they're a parent, a friend, or a husband. Whether as pieces of a cherished remote past or reminders of a loss, the letters left behind by the people we care about, and who have cared about us, alternate between comforting and inflicting pain, or sometimes do both at once. Their power to move and evoke is out of all proportion to their physical dimensions.

In January 2008, my sister and I visited the Georgia O'Keeffe archive in Santa Fe. This elegant institution proved to be an outsized reliquary enshrining the painter's possessions, including her library, some articles of clothing, brushes, palettes, and collections of her own beloved relics: feathers, shells, bones. The visit was a perfect occasion to ponder how an artist's or anybody's personal life and career are remembered and preserved: what is saved, and how, and why?

In the Drawer

I can only bear to go
        through your old letters glancingly at first.
        Tucked away in my own files,
they were half forgotten and half lost.

Georgia O'Keeffe's blue sneakers, navy blazer,
        and white silk handkerchief turn out to have
        been reverently preserved in Santa Fe
in cabinets (my sister took me there today)

whose shallow drawers contain, with other treasures,
        paint chips like little shards of desert sky;

brushes: pastels. Open another: stones
which she collected, cherished. Another: bones,

vertebrae especially, and skulls
    small enough to fit into these long low drawers;
    another, rows of pink and pearly shells.
A reliquary of the whole outdoors,

of desert seasons shrunk and tucked away
    in shallow trays that shut without a sound
    and open only at some scholar's "Sesame."
Such objects, if they can be said to speak,

employ a different dialect from the bright
    gloss of colors stroked across a canvas
    affably beckoning from some neutral wall,
so that the viewer peers into it as

into a mirror that can tell whatever
    it is we ask reflections to convey.
    Bones and shells and stones, though, keep their counsel.
As to what your letters to me say,

I cannot yet quite bear to look and see.
    I do note shared jokes, references, joy,
    when I snatch a glance
quickly, from the corner of my eye.

Finally and little by little, early in 2009, I began to reread
the letters. It still wasn't easy, but it was hugely rewarding.
More graphically, in a way, than snapshots, the letters present
exactly what George used to be, bringing back the qualities
that he has lost: the ability to write a complicated, witty sentence; curiosity about and interest in other people; the constant
urge to move forward with his own work; the undercurrent of
concern for me and for Jonathan.

Even a glance at the letters reminds me how hungry George
was, when we first met, for someone to talk to, someone who

would listen well and tell her own story back. It took me quite a long time to realize that the customary conversational rhythm of talking, listening, and answering was somehow askew in George's family, particularly when he was with his brother and sister. Some of the siblings clammed up; others monologued. Interruptions abounded; no one seemed to listen very carefully or be curious about anyone else. George's mother was a notable exception to this pattern, but her stroke in 1979, only two years after I met her, effectively silenced her. Her fate—to live on for twenty-two years essentially without talking—now seems very likely to befall George as well. But I have his letters, and I will pass them on to Jonathan.

In the pre-email days of the 1980s and 90s, George's letters to me and mine to him were an effortless continuation of our conversation when one of us was away. Our lively exchange began as soon as we met and didn't flag until sometime in the late 1990s. If I can dispel the fog of the last decade, the letters will let me recover the cheerful, funny, thoughtful man I fell in love with. They are instruments to break the spell of silence. By bringing the past to life, they help me fight back against the phenomenon described by Sherwin Nuland in *How We Die* when he writes: "A life that has been well lived and a shared sense of happiness and accomplishment are ever after seen through the smudged glass of the last few years." There is much truth in Nuland's words. Still, reading old letters helps to wipe the glass clean again.

Here are some passages organized by topic rather than date. I am guilty of not always knowing which piece he's referring to when he writes about the process of composing.

> [He's describing some fellow colonists at MacDowell. One, Andrea Fisher, I myself had known earlier.]
> . . . this left the field free for ping-pong & for prolonged chat with Andrea, among others. You're right about one thing; she really is smart. She listens like a cat, picking up on things

people don't even realize they've said. (In this she's the opposite of Helen Nearing, whose main conversational gambit is asking a question you had given the answer to in your previous sentence.) . . .

★ ★ ★

I had a good but hard day of work today—hard because I spent the first 2 hours or so on stuff the piece rejected as though it were an organ transplant; good because I then sketched and drafted a lot the piece will accept, and because the piece is beginning to take on a life independent of my intentions.

★ ★ ★

I continued work on the 2nd mvt today until I hit a snag in the early afternoon. Then I got together all the sketches [of] the first movement, indexed them, and began a very detailed (which is not to say final) draft of the first 12 seconds. It doesn't sound like much, but with this beginning, which is in a sense very simple, the devil really *is* in the details, since there are so many ways the general idea—moving from a sort of compressed chaos into something more shaped and formal—could be realized. As for the essay, it has a long way to go. My main impression going over my notes is seeing how incredibly much I've learned about its subject over the past 18 months . . .

I've been playing some Bach and a lot of Chopin—no need to send any more music.

I'll get this ready to send now, have a glass of wine, play the piano, & plan to do two things I haven't done yet: go to bed early & read before bed in my room.

★ ★ ★

Switched to the 3rd movement, which is also going well (the 2nd went well yesterday). I'm off in a few minutes to do my laundry, but expect to come back later to work some more & finish this. I envy Andrea, who stays up late, sleeps late, reads, thinks & draws a bit, then hangs out—a life of leisure caused in part by not wanting to have to take anything heavy back to England. I'm much more compulsive, & am always prepared for a sitzkrieg—knowing that if I keep at it something always seems to come.

★   ★   ★

You ask about the dialogic character of the piece. Well first, each of the instruments has a different persona, and is associated with a different interval collection I can best describe by associating each with a composer: flute—Debussy; oboe—Varese; clarinet—Messiaen/Stravinsky; violin—Ives/ Copland/Americana; viola—Schoenberg op 33A; cello— Webern; percussion—a bit of a minimalist, (but) tends to follow the dominant trend. They interact in a variety of ways. For examples: the violin and cello collections can share four pitches, fight over the two pairs of different pitches that would complete both collections; the whole ensemble can be dominated by the collection associated with one instrument, while each individually still tries to assert its own collection; the instruments can imitate each others' gestures, translating them into their own collection; they can exchange masks . . .

★   ★   ★

I've discovered that by sitting at Louise Talma's table one gets a higher level of conversation than elsewhere. Not that she says much: mostly just grunts of disagreement or an occasional stifled laugh. She's about to be 89, and obviously finds it physically difficult to say more than a few words at a time. The longest sentence I've heard from her was "Someone took the ice tray from Eaves"—rivaled only by (contradicting me) "Sussmeyer was no student." In this crowd of virtuous people, she stands out for smoking (quite restricted here both in theory & in practice) & having a large bourbon before dinner. After initially finding it hard to control, I've come to love the piano at Veltin. It's not 'forgiving' (as our Sewanee friend would say)—if you try to play a piece you don't know well, it punishes you. But once you learn it, it rewards you with all kinds of beautiful things you didn't realize you meant.

★   ★   ★

On the way out here before dinner I saw something moving, turned on my flashlight, and saw a doe and two fauns [sic] lope across the field! No catamounts (it seems the woman who wrote the cat book was twice a colonist, had a fight with someone on the staff, & has been bad-mouthing the colony ever since).

★ ★ ★

After going to town in mid-afternoon, I finished *Swann in Love*, and reviewed my notes on it (also composed). What amazed me, given the way I'm reading Proust this time, is how almost purely visual Swann's imagination is compared with that of the narrator. His references to smell, taste, or the sense of touch are incredibly few and mostly conventional or derogatory. Perhaps you can tell me: do orchids have a smell? Chrysanthemums? He never "hears" space; he's said to have a "taste for good cooking," but we never get any details (the tea he gets chez Odette is merely "cloudy"). For him, sight is the only sense that does not "escape our intelligence."

★ ★ ★

Speaking of Swann, Nattiez (*Proust as Musician*) asks entirely the wrong question: "Why, given that Swann is in so many ways like the narrator, does Swann not become an artist, too?" He tries to answer the question (which might better be "why doesn't Swann ever accomplish anything at all," not (if I remember correctly) even an essay on Vermeer) by comparing Swann's programmatic (and visual) relation to the Vinteuil sonata with the narrator's more "absolute" relation to it. But the problem with Swann is that (as becomes explicit about 300 pages into *Within a Budding Grove*), sight—being too tied to intellect and to habit—is not a sense which gives us access to involuntary memory . . .

★ ★ ★

You've made a couple of remarks about not knowing what my Wagner-Proust essay was to be about, remarks I haven't followed up because I needed to read Proust again before I could be sure I had a subject. I still can't put it very well and am sure that it will change a lot before I even begin writing. But it has something to do with Wagner's attempt to have every aspect of the drama, down to the smallest details of staging & lighting reinforce the same points simultaneously: you SEE it on stage, you HEAR the characters talking about it and you hear it represented in the music. I'm sure (*a la* Huxley) he would have had you smell it if he could have! This seemed (and seems) to me very similar to Proust's imagery, which tries to involve every sense simultaneously, almost to the point of synesthesia . . .

There is much, much more. I don't think he ever wrote the proposed Wagner-Proust essay; the letters constitute the makings of yet another essay. And even if they don't, they have the wonderful quality of sending me back both to the text and the music, and also of giving me a picture of George's mind at work: remembering, comparing, questioning, savoring.

In September 2008, George moved from White Plains to the Eightieth Street Residence in Manhattan. While packing his belongings, I found a stray sheet of yellow legal paper somewhere in his room. It was in his handwriting and had his name at the top. I tried to imagine the circumstances under which he had written it: An attempt at a journal? Some sort of cognitive exercise led by an activities coordinator—an assignment perhaps, to describe a picture George was being shown? I'll never know. I can only be sure that this was written sometime between January and September 2008. George carries his book of essays around like a talisman; I seem to need to keep this piece of paper near me. Sometimes when people ask how George is doing I have the impulse to show it to them. If they are people I like and trust, sometimes I do show it to them. The next page shows what it looks like.

George Edwards

a windfell such a prace in the fall There a : 1: The fall of

Firw is of a Trind fell : a yand froge in the full, annd £ comm full a VINN fall of comm of a comm Bisan of am for misshng of a piw of a heet too an Comminyssina of a commnshindle at ffirns al finnge — but it first but of T Sonn as a excuss for the disinn Tterre mnina, or a a for a fullenn Tirm — entning fortoore, as inetiring to inter mmennnnt.

chiny in ton each you, so y yoon until I wuy oone to as ws --- way tanny as in yall wass

In a sense each These buy Y is in in a a less amore sens sensee in more less The less morre The my more the producte --- eache; yoeache is each of its initialial.

CHAPTER 26

A Pain Somewhere
in the Room

One cloudy Sunday afternoon in April 2008, I went to a concert of new music.

It was the first contemporary music concert I had attended since Columbia's farewell for George more than two years earlier. From the start of George's illness, or at least since the time he stopped teaching, I had been giving myself permission to ignore, if not positively dislike, contemporary music. Back when George and I were first together, I put in ample hours at sparsely attended events, and even enjoyed some aspects of them. There had been an energy present, the electricity of hopeful anticipation. Goodness knows how many world premieres I heard—not only George's pieces but also works of many other composers. I can remember being almost as excited as George was to hear the first strains of a piece of his that had never before been performed. I usually liked the beginnings and endings of George's compositions, but I tended to get lost in the middle. Sometimes I liked other composers' work too, but not much stays with me at this distance; my memory focuses on words.

This April concert did feature words. It consisted of vocal settings, by a handful of contemporary composers, of poems by Dana Gioia, an acquaintance of mine of twenty years' standing. None of the music did much for me, or indeed, so far as I could tell, for Dana's poems; the renderings seemed unsubtle. I thought of George's intricate, delicate chamber pieces, and of his few vocal settings, intricate and complex settings, by this self-proclaimed atheist, of poems by George Herbert and Gerard Manley Hopkins. The last poem George set, around 1993, was Walt Whitman's too little known masterpiece, "This Compost," a poem about mortality and rebirth; the title of George's piece, taken from a line in the poem, was "The Resurrection of the Wheat." The soprano who had commissioned this piece complained that she couldn't learn its difficult rhythms. George struggled all one summer to finish it, but it has never been performed.

People sometimes ask me whether George ever set any of my poems. He never did, and I don't think I ever expected him to. But I do remember, when he was setting several Hopkins poems, in the summer of 1977, his asking me to read him "Pied Beauty" over and over again. I think he wanted to know how I heard the rhythms. In late August, that same summer, he set Hopkins's little poem "Heaven-Haven" in a single afternoon. George's Hopkins settings are among the pieces of his I best remember and most cherish.

Back to April 2008. To be underwhelmed by hearing live performances of contemporary music, including many world premieres, was far from a new experience. Beginning in 1976, I had sat through countless concerts, and my sense of general disappointment now was like an old acquaintance I hadn't seen in a while but remembered perfectly. What did feel odd (though when I came to think of it, not surprising) was that one of the singers and one of the composers at this Gioia event were people whose names and faces I knew. Even though this concert had nothing to do with Columbia—it took place in the auditorium of the Guggenheim Museum—such connections, in the small world of contemporary music, were to be expected.

All the same, at the reception following the concert, it felt strange to be in the same apartment, in the same buffet line, as these two people. They had known George in the past, knew some of his work. Did they now know that he was ill? Doubtful; the grapevine in the new music world, or at least at George's end of it, seems rather balky and tardy. On the other hand, it's a place I don't belong to, so how should I know? For the past decade George had been steadily withdrawing from it, as from every other circle he belonged to, so it would stand to reason that people would lose track of him. In any event, whether or not they knew anything about George's condition, this soprano and this composer had no clue who I was. I felt invisible. A momentary fantasy unfolded: cross the room, introduce myself, and tell them what was wrong with George, snagging a couple of unwilling revelers to unburden myself of my load of bad news by passing it on.

The fantasy faded in less time than it takes to write it down. But the uncomfortable feeling of invisibility that triggered it is what keeps that strange Sunday afternoon alive in my memory.

The afternoon stays with me for another reason, too. My kind friend Lorna, who also attended the concert and the reception, had wondered, she told me later, whether the event would be painful for me. She had feared that it would bring back memories of earlier, happier times. When Lorna told me this, my first thought was that she had far more delicate sensibilities than I, who seemed to have developed a tough, unsentimental carapace. Listening to the settings of Dana's poems, I had suffered nothing worse than an attack of drowsiness.

But of course that wasn't quite true. If the concert itself was not uncomfortable, then the party after it decidedly was. The sensation of invisibility wasn't new, but it was unexpected, and it carried a familiar, even if temporary, sense of desolate loneliness. There was pain there, of a sort; but it wasn't precisely my pain. Thinking about it, I was reminded of Mrs. Gradgrind's deathbed answer to her daughter Louisa in Dickens's *Hard*

Times. Louisa has asked her mother if she is in pain. "'I think there's a pain somewhere in the room,' said Mrs. Gradgrind, 'but I couldn't positively say that I have got it.'"

My friend was right after all: the concert did cause pain. It did remind me of what I had lost. The loss was twofold: first, the loss of experiences such as sitting next to George in Miller Theatre or Merkin Concert Hall sharing his anticipation; then, the loss of the comfortable sense that such scenes would go on repeating themselves with variations as far as the mind could roam—that there would be more compositions, more concerts, more premieres. In other words, what I had lost was a shared past and a shared future.

Once the concert was over, there was also the oddness— not altogether unpleasant, but still new—of coming home from a social gathering and finding myself alone. For years, living with George had been lonely; living without him was lonely in a different way. Back in the apartment after the concert and the party, back in the bedroom, I looked around. Nothing had changed. Or else, though the change was nearly invisible, everything had changed.

CHAPTER 27

In the Middest

It's the middle of August 2008. I've been at our house in Vermont since early July, and since the middle of July, George has been here too. My son and his girlfriend, Waverly, picked him up from the place where he's been living since January and drove him up here. Next week—not that he knows this yet—they'll drive him back.

So for the past several weeks we have all been together here in the house. How on earth to describe this time? A spate of contradictory adjectives doesn't quite capture how confusing it has been—and even more confusing (if possible) to think about than to live through. These are some of the words that come to mind: poignant and matter-of-fact; relaxing and exhausting; triumphant, risky; happy, sad; unlikely, inevitable. Can one feel these things all at once, or only one at a time?

In many ways, I have loved these weeks of rain, washed-out roads, good meals, Cabot cheese, misty mornings, dawn dreams. (Why are dreams in the country so rich and detailed?) Lately I've loved the ripening blackberries and apples, the full moon, and even our poor cat Cleo's getting skunked. I love having my son, Jonathan, and his beautiful, strong, energetic, devoted girlfriend here. I love to look at them and listen to them. Their voices remind me, even as they correct it, of the essential silence I've lived with for so long. I love their cooking and cleanup, and their boundless social energy—

we've sat down seven, eight, or nine to lunch or dinner four or five times.

Together with Jeff, the tattooed, mustachioed, earringed aide who comes in his pickup truck for a few hours each weekday, Jon and Wave and I have been able to lift and sustain the weight of George almost effortlessly. No one of us carries too much of the burden.

But the burden is still there. Jon and Waverly have taken George to the Danville courts to play tennis as often as the wet weather has permitted. When he isn't playing tennis or ping-pong, eating breakfast, lunch, or dinner, or sitting on the porch smoking a cigarette, George is an all-but-unspeaking, restless presence. He sits in his big, brown chair, looking expectantly at no one in particular. He doesn't settle: every so often, he gets up and walks through the back door to the compost heap or the berry patch, or pads upstairs to lie down. He moves silently; when you turn your head, he's not there.

Part of the burden lies in the confusing, cat-and-mouse game of figure and ground. Which is the more important here? Does the habit of many years trump disability? Does disability blight habit? Do they simply exist side by side, or does one slip behind the other and out of sight? It's so familiar for George to be here—familiar for him, familiar for us. Does that make it natural and appropriate? It feels good to him, I think—not that he seems especially happy.

The alternation between foreground and background, all played out against George's ghostly silence, reminds me of Wallace Stevens's poem "The Snow Man," whose spectral speculations might be said, if anything can, to capture this summer's elusive texture. I'm thinking especially of the end of the poem, where the listener, "nothing himself," beholds "nothing that is not there and the nothing that is." That has often felt like the choice I've been facing—no, living.

But this peculiar rural interlude seems like something out of fiction rather than poetry. Frank Kermode, whose *The Sense of an Ending* I have lately been consulting in search of help with this unmapped, unresolved feeling, writes, "We cannot . . . be denied an end; it is one of the great charms of books that they have to end." Accordingly, novelizing these weeks may be a way of providing closure, or at least envisioning closure, for a situation that in fact doesn't offer any.

By "novelizing" I mean thinking of life in terms of literature. True, books from the discipline of psychology, books about dementia, books like Pauline Boss's *Ambiguous Loss* also speak to this open-endedness, this lack of closure. But literary criticism, like poetry, sometimes phrases things more suggestively, does a more convincing job of sketching an absence, conjuring an end.

This week in late August in Vermont is not an end—far from it. Or rather, any end, such as the end of this summer, closing the house, returning to the city, will lead to other beginnings. People "in the middest," as Kermode observes, "make considerable imaginative investments in coherent patterns which, by the provision of an end, make possible a satisfying consonance with the origins and the middle." Absent these imaginative investments in patterns, endings are always problematic. Summer drawing toward a close in the country, however customary it ought to feel, seems especially fraught; one senses the encroaching shadow of autumn, the built-in term limits, the inexorable sentence. If anything, I used to feel, let the end approach less deliberately—let's get the waiting, the elegiac suspension, over with! I think it was in late summer of 2002, as August was slowly ending and Jonathan's departure for college slowly approaching (at least these processes seemed slow at the time), that I wrote a fretful little poem called "Snake."

Ends: of summer; time in the country; time
before departures. Time
tapers to a snake that slides invisibly

off into the long grass of the world,
though such a narrowed notion fails to scratch
the itch lodged in between
impatiently waiting for something new to happen
and clinging to what, having
already happened, slithers
off into the brush without a sound.

When I try to provide a coherent pattern for the ending of the summer of 2008, I come up with something like a pastoral epilogue—a pivotal moment of ending and renewal. If Jon and Waverly had a baby, for example, the reconfigured family constellation might recall the end of *Howards End* or even *War and Peace*. After the *Sturm und Drang*, births trump deaths; a new generation makes its appearance. In this household there has been no death, at least no literal death. But perhaps instead of playing a ghost, George can stand in for the baby. Certainly his aide functions very effectively as a babysitter. When the aide, Jeff, pulls up in his pickup truck, Jon, Wave, and I feel free to peel off and do whatever we want to do. In the routine that's developed, I usually hop into my rental car and drive the few miles over back roads to my friend Reeve Lindbergh's guest house, a Swiss-style chalet Reeve built in 1991 for her mother, Anne Morrow Lindbergh. Here in the Mouse House, as the family call it, I can perch on a stool and write at the kitchen counter. I can lie on a sofa and nap or gaze out the window. Or I can sit on the veranda in a wicker chair and look down the driveway, only 200 yards, to Reeve and her husband Nat's farmhouse and barn, with the sheep-dotted hills beyond. I can be alone with my thoughts.

The last few years of Mrs. Lindbergh's life, when she was suffering from dementia, she lived in this house, with twenty-four-hour care. Reeve could walk down the driveway to visit her mother, but they weren't under the same roof. Reeve had imagined that after her mother's death, she would use the house as a place in which to write, but she found that she didn't care to spend much time there—a feeling I think I understand. I am eternally grateful to Reeve and her husband for the gift of space and time. No matter how tired or distracted I am, there is something sustaining and focusing about the Mouse House— its welcoming (not spectral) silence; its friendly emptiness.

Most likely, it was at one of my respites in the Mouse House that I began to think about a happy ending to the summer— not to replace our reality with such a conclusion, but rather to realize the unavailability of a conclusion. Kermode describes a happy ending as "the old ending that panders to temporal expectations, the sort described (in its comic mode) by Henry James as a 'distribution at the last of prizes, pensions, husbands, wives, babies, millions, appended paragraphs, and cheerful remarks.'" It sounds so tidy! Life never ends as neatly as a novel. Does it end at all? Faulkner: "The past is never over. It isn't even past."

One lives life a moment at a time. Here are a few moments from that summer: I'm walking with George around the Triangle, the hilly road we live on that links many neighboring houses and the brook known as the Water Andric. We've been walking this route in the summer for thirty years. George may not say a word for the whole walk; he may comment on the mist rising across the valley: "Misty!" He walks much faster than I do—he walks faster than anyone—but he pauses from time to time and looks back at me. Expectantly? Affectionately? Hard to say. Sometimes I avoid his eye; sometimes we smile at each other.

Here we are playing ping-pong. He laughs—with pleasure? I used to think so, but lately his laughter has come to seem more like a general conversational move, a gesture that just says, "Here I am."

He goes to bed at about eight o'clock and sleeps for twelve hours. The night he and Jon and Wave arrived, I went to bed in the guest room, thinking that to sleep in the same bed with

George would confuse us both. But I couldn't sleep. Eventually I crawled into bed with him and slept soundly. George's sleep had always helped me sleep better, and apparently it still did. As always in the country, I found that I dreamed a lot, or remembered dreams more clearly. Especially near dawn, my dreams were often most vivid, but also confused and full of trouble. I seemed to be taking a retrospective tour of my own life.

Dreams in a Damp House

July. Now August. Damp old house in the country.
Crowded into the last sweet hour of sleep,

characters from strata of my past
stroll through walk-on parts dawn after grey dawn.

Here's my first husband. Here's the carpenter
who laid the floor boards in the living room.

The floor later caved in. There was no foundation.
Could he really have put bare wood over dank earth?

Here is my sister-in-law, the family archivist,
chipping away at an archaeological site.

Here from a raw and sore and recent layer
and writhing on a bed of indecision

is an ex-friend caught painfully between
present, past, and future. As am I:

for here you are, familiar and impassive
bedmate I snuggle against as I busily dream.

You are my past, or thirty years of it.
Last week that anniversary came and went.

But present? Future? Now that we again
are sleeping side by side, I've lost my bearings.

The warm rampart your body I know well;
not so well its silent denizen.

Yet here we are in this damp house together.
Friends who don't understand, or friends who do,

constantly ask whether you recognize me.
I am not sure I recognize you.

When I get up in the morning, I always try to be swift and silent, hoping George will go on sleeping for a couple of hours. But almost always he gets up soon after I do, dresses himself (he may pull on a pair of my way-too-short pants, wear a T-shirt backward or inside out, but he generally does pretty well), comes silently downstairs, and looks expectant. Another day begins. We listen to the news on Vermont Public Radio. George still rolls his eyes at the sentimental strains of music that precede Garrison Keillor's "Writer's Almanac."

The empty hours go by. "Do you still play the piano?" George's cousin John asked when he and his family visited last week. "Yes." "Do you still compose?" "Yes." Are these answers accurate? No.

I can't sum these weeks up, I can't analyze them, I can't parse them at all. They happened. I'm glad they happened. Am I glad they're almost over? It's always a wistful time when summer draws to a close. I feel bad that George will return to where he was before; I feel relieved; I feel tired. Will future summers continue to feature such visits? At least for the foreseeable future, maybe they will.

"When we survive," writes Kermode in *The Sense of an Ending*, "we make little images of moments which have seemed like ends." Insofar as this summer in Vermont has been like a novel, it has been, in a bittersweet way, a novel with a happy ending—or a happy lack of ending.

It has also been a novel with, if not a moral, at least a lesson: I still sleep better next to George.

Vertical and Horizontal

Slowly you've been sinking out of sight.
You're losing the ability to speak.
I miss you, though, when I lie down at night,

No rage against the dying of the light.
The sun still shines. But something's sprung a leak.
Gradually you're vanishing from sight.

We no longer converse, but I still write.
During the day I teach, which means I talk.
But I miss you when I lie down at night.

Your body hasn't changed. Yet though your height
is still 6'4", you are diminished; weak.
Slowly you are sinking out of sight.

No gods, no reasons, nothing to placate.
Habit's force, which keeps me on my track,
makes me miss you every single night.

You striding on, me panting, yelling "Wait!":
all those summers, that was how we'd walk.
Now you are slowly fading from my sight
I miss you, still, when I lie down at night.

CHAPTER 28

A Meeting Place
of Multiple Presences

Monday, August 25, 2008. Two days ago I returned to the city from Vermont.

The usual piles of mail awaited me. I went for the books first: some I had ordered recently, some I'd ordered back in early July before leaving town and had forgotten. Among this latter group was Jamaica Kincaid's *My Brother*, which a friend had strongly recommended. I opened the book and started reading Kincaid's account of her brother's death from AIDS, admiring both her relentless honesty and her ability to slip back and forth in time in a complicated narrative.

Very early on, Kincaid writes, "At the time the phone call came telling me of my brother's illness, among the many comforts, luxuries that I enjoyed was reading a book." She proceeds to describe the book, a gardening book, and her thoughts about it, so that when the phone call with its freight of bad news arrives, the meditative mood is rudely shattered for us, her readers, as it was for her.

At the moment *my* phone rang, I was alternating between rooting around in Kincaid's book and typing up a syllabus for the MFA poetry workshop I was due to start teaching at Rutgers right after Labor Day. I was also waiting for a phone call, though it was still fairly early in the afternoon and I didn't expect it quite yet. Nevertheless I was alert, on the edge of my chair. Today was the day Jonathan and Waverly were driving George back from Vermont to Hearthstone, the facility in White Plains they had picked him up from a few weeks earlier. The young people were giving me the huge gift of taking George away from the familiar place and freedom of the country to—well, would it be the familiarity of the place he'd been living in since January?

It was Jon on his cell phone, and his voice sounded tight. They had pulled up in front of Hearthstone and were about to take George upstairs, but he was rebellious, desperate, trying to run or walk rapidly down the street. Dad won't go back there, Jon said. Would I talk to him? No, I said, I wouldn't. I told him I had nothing to say that could help. I said I would call the people at Hearthstone so they could come downstairs and help shepherd George back in. I didn't say Jon should have called them as he and Wave were approaching the place. I think I assumed he would know this, or even assumed I had already said it. But I suppose the reentry would have been difficult in any case.

Jon didn't demur or plead. He did say that the situation wasn't physically or psychologically easy, and we hung up. I called Hearthstone, and the people in charge there said they would dispatch a nurse and an aide to go downstairs and intercept George. I gave them Jon's phone number and settled in to wait. There was no point in calling Jon again, or calling anyone. They all had their hands full—everyone, maybe, except me. This crisis, I thought to myself, would be resolved soon. Or else it wouldn't.

"How did I feel?" Kincaid writes later in her book, at one of the points that punctuated her brother's decline. "I did not know how I felt. I was a combustion of feelings." Without losing any of its authority, her poised voice admits to a swirl of confusion. And she's telling the truth: at such moments one doesn't have the luxury of knowing how one feels.

There were many feelings, none pleasant. I felt guilty—not only for reinserting George into that place but also for not being able to help my son and his girlfriend at this bad moment. Guilty and ineffective, inadequate and selfish on at least two levels, then, vis-à-vis my husband and my son. I also felt pulled, as in a nightmare, back into the world of crisis, coercion, waiting, waiting, waiting, the world I had been inhabiting on and off between January and June: phone calls, dilemmas, standing by, doing what could or had to be done. Perhaps there was one slightly pleasant feeling: gratitude that this particular thorny episode was out of my hands, that others were having to cope.

When you're waiting, time is transformed. Like silence, time can feel loose or tight, gracious or painful, noticeable or invisible. Waiting in alert suspense felt like a familiar throbbing. I also felt stretched, again in a familiar way, between the apartment to which I was beginning to get rehabituated and the street in White Plains where Hearthstone was—and then upstairs to the fifth floor. Somewhere on the sidewalk or in the lobby, in the elevator or upstairs, this drama was being acted. Reenacted.

There was nothing to do but wait. I finished my syllabus and turned off the computer. Paced around, lit some incense, put on the timer. There would be no point in calling Jon or Hearthstone for an hour. The phone rang once, twice, three times at intervals of ten minutes or so. Each time I'd leap to answer it, and each time it turned out to be telemarketers for charities I'd idiotically donated to in the past, the kind that try to sell you light bulbs or garbage bags or cleaning fluid for an exorbitant amount. I can't talk, I said each time, I have a family crisis. (No doubt they hear that line all the time.) The minutes ticked away.

After forty minutes or so, the downstairs doorbell rang. I jumped, the cats jumped. An image popped into my mind of

Jonathan at the door with his father, the two tall men looming in the threshold, George confused, furious at me, but unbudgeably home henceforth. This turn of events seemed not far-fetched but entirely possible, even probable. Wasn't Jon somewhat ambivalent about his father's being in an institution, and weren't we all, at this point, ambivalent about Hearthstone? Had Jon taken matters into his own hands and just driven his father home? Could they already be parked outside? Was George's time away from home over? Had all the painful struggle to get him into Hearthstone been for nothing? Thoughts tumbled over each other. I grabbed my keys and raced down three flights of stairs.

It was the UPS man with a package for me. Ilya, the building's eccentric Russian part-time doorman, likes to ring a piercing and superfluous peal on the downstairs bell to announce the arrival of packages. Mentally cursing this habit of Ilya's, I took the box out of the deliveryman's hands—he was waiting by the elevator—and scuttled back up the stairs to the blessedly empty apartment.

Tearing at the layers of cardboard and tape with shaking hands, I managed to pry open the package. It was a newly published book, Rosanna Warren's *Fables of the Self: Studies in Lyric Poetry*. This wasn't the moment to open the book, but I'd been aware it was coming out and had looked forward to reading it. I unfolded the publicity flyer that was enclosed and read a quote from the author: "The self is a locus, a meeting place of multiple presences organized, in the individual person, by will, experience, and character, while the authorial self in the work of literature is organized by rhetorical structures and patterned language."

Actually, on that first gulped reading, I didn't get past the word "character." I didn't manage the transition from life to literature; I was stuck in life. I was hooked on that phrase about the self as a meeting place of multiple presences. How could I not be? My own life at that moment was a traffic jam of presences—or in Kincaid's more vivid phrase, a combustion of feelings.

To the guilt and anxiety and pity, the regret and fear and suspense, which had begun to assail me simultaneously the moment Jon called, I could now add the ugly little snarl of another emotion: envy. Back in the early days after George's diagnosis, I used to envy the companionship, the apparent contentment, of married couples who had conversations. Happily married couples still cause me the occasional pang, but that form of envy has eased a good deal. This was a different kind of envy. I envied Rosanna, whom I've known and respected for many years, for having managed to write and publish the elegant, meditative book (I knew it would be these things even before I read it) that I held in my hands. She had written it, I thought angrily, while I was struggling with the exhausting day-to-day matters of George's care and the even more daunting larger issues that care entailed. Never mind that I knew very well Rosanna's life had plenty of challenges; for the moment, envy trumped my sense of balance. And more: over my envy of her accomplishment was layered the unpleasant patina of self-pity. Poor me, having to deal with George's illness forever and ever, year after slow year—the ups and downs, the loneliness, the distraction, the thanklessness, the expense, the grinding slowness.

The self as a locus, a meeting place of multiple presences: Rosanna certainly had that right. My head felt like an unruly committee meeting. Will, experience, and character? I wasn't so sure about the will part. Some experiences are beyond or contrary to what we may will.

We all survived that afternoon. Jon and Waverly, with some help from the Hearthstone staff, managed to get George upstairs there and spend some fairly peaceful time with him before they left. I'd been planning to go to a support group that evening, but life trumped self-help, and instead (it was a no-brainer) I took Jon and Wave out to dinner. We were all shaken.

Later on, when I was calmer, I reconsidered the second half of Rosanna's formulation about the self, which I had been too impatient to take in when I'd torn open her book's cardboard wrapping with trembling hands. In contrast to the self that's a locus of multiple presences, she writes, "the authorial self in the work of literature is organized by rhetorical structures and patterned language." No arguments there. Only, under the pressure of the moment, a bleak little thought. The author, it seemed to me, always had a choice: not only a choice of what rhetorical structures and what patterned language to deploy, but the larger choice of whether to be an authorial self—an author—at all. The self as a meeting place of multiple presences, on the other hand, has no choice; it simply is. Amid the clashing rocks of obligations, life has to be lived. I chose to marry George, but I never chose the way our lives would turn out. I did, however, choose to be a writer, and though squeezed by the conditions of my life, I am still in charge of what I write. I also chose (and this applies to Rosanna) to be a reading self. In fact, when a dire phone call came, it was likely to interrupt me, as Jamaica Kincaid had been interrupted, in the process of reading.

Jamaica Kincaid had received bad news and had captured the experience in her book with such candor and power that her words spoke to me in the middle of an episode in my own life. Later, when I was able to reflect, I realized that countless people had managed to weather crises partly by writing about them. What they wrote had helped others; but first of all it helped the writers themselves.

Back to my syllabus. School starts next week.

CHAPTER 29

Suave Mari Magno

School was about to begin; my first class was going to be September 2, 2008, the day after Labor Day. George was back where he was. I blithely assumed—what did I assume? That life would go on predictably; that the beginning of the semester would coincide with the end of an ambiguous summer and the resumption of academic rhythms. One set of things would end, another set would begin. As Frank Kermode says, we cannot be denied an ending.

But some endings are provisional. George had been back in White Plains for less than a week when all sense of an orderly ending ended. On Sunday, August 31, Jon and I had a guest over for brunch, my friend Adrianne from Athens, who was in town to insert her daughter into college at the New School. The next day would be Labor Day; the day after that, I'd start teaching; and a few days after that, on Sunday, September 7, Jonathan would board the first of several flights en route to Nepal, where he was to spend a year on a Fulbright fellowship.

We were all enjoying popovers, jam, and coffee when the phone rang. It was one of the nurses at Hearthstone, with the message that George had pushed someone who had wandered into his room. The intruder, a frail old man, had fallen down and hadn't been able to get up. He had been taken to the hospital for evaluation.

I'm so sorry, I said, or words to that effect. Is there anything I can do? Keep me posted.

Something like this had happened before. Back in May, George had briefly had a roommate at Hearthstone and had tried to push him. Fortunately the roommate's grown son happened to be visiting at the time; he was able not only to report the incident but also to ward off any actual attack. The upshot was that the roommate moved to another room (and soon to another facility) and George spent Memorial Day weekend in the psychiatric ward of a White Plains hospital for observation. I visited him there on a lovely leafy day. I'd never been to a locked ward before. I walked down the corridor: various drugged-looking patients were sitting in armchairs or leaning against the walls. As if he had stepped into the wrong movie, George was pacing impatiently, alertly back and forth at the end of the hall.

"What am I doing here?" he asked me. "Get me out of here."

"Honey, you're here because you had a little trouble with your roommate, remember?"

He did remember. "Interloper!" he growled.

That hospital stay was mercifully short. But now, a few months later, George had been intruded upon by another interloper.

It transpired that while he was away in Vermont, the new management of Hearthstone had reshuffled some of the residents' assigned rooms. George's new room—the room to which he had reluctantly gone the week before, when Jon and Wave brought him back from Vermont—was located in what had formerly been the Hearthstone director's office, where residents had tended to congregate, often drifting in when the door was open. The old man who had crossed George's threshold had almost certainly been confused. George too was undoubtedly confused, not to mention agitated and unhappy at having been brought back from Vermont not only to this place but to a new room. As became crystal clear a bit later, the situation was a recipe for trouble. Is dementia an especially favorable environment for twenty-twenty hindsight, or does any kind of human trouble foster this uncomfortable phenomenon?

The next day, Labor Day, I got another call. The old man whom George pushed had a broken pelvis. Too frail to be a candidate for surgery, he might never walk again. Appalled, I apologized again, and enquired what might result from this—could it be called an accident? In the jargon of the business, "incident" would probably be the word of choice.

"Oh, I don't think anyone blames George," said the nurse on the line, or whoever was on duty that Labor Day.

Did I wonder if this could really be true? I should have, and perhaps briefly I did, but I had too much on my mind to think about it very hard: the start of school, Jonathan's imminent departure. But (surprise) next day in my office, I received the third call in three days. As in a fairy tale, there was something magical, something decisively clinching, about this third event. This time it was the interim director of Hearthstone, who announced that the decision had been made that George would have to leave.

Many, many conversations took place in the next few days that I no longer remember, or want to remember, clearly. I did see Hearthstone's point of view. I could imagine how the other man's family must feel. There was no one to blame, in one sense. In another, there was plenty of blame to go around. What was indisputable was that George had to leave a place I was by now eager to get him out of, and that the timing of this crisis was terrible. (Is such timing ever good?) The bad news call came at about ten o'clock in the morning while I was in my office on the first day of school—preparing to meet with my two graduate teaching assistants before teaching, early that afternoon, the first class of a course on children's literature in which eighty students were enrolled.

I got through the day. How? Habit—automatic pilot—and human help both played a part. I went to my sympathetic chair's office, told her the situation, briefly wept. I told my sympathetic young TAs and didn't weep. I built a wall down the middle of my brain and taught the class. Mercifully, Jonathan still had the rest of the week at home, and there was time to debrief and discuss and plan. Mercifully too, and to me astonishingly, not only did there soon turn out to be a place that was more suitable, but this place was the one I had visited three times, the most recent time with Jonathan back in July. The final good surprise was that the Eightieth Street Residence would have a room for George by mid-September.

What strikes me now (again the twenty-twenty hindsight phenomenon) is my pattern of doing what needed to be done before I knew it needed to be done, without consciously acknowledging any urgency in the situation and without a mental timetable. Back in the spring of 2007, for example, I hadn't said to myself, "I can only stand this situation for another six months"; I'd simply started checking out a few places. When I finally moved George in January 2008, I had made the decision only a couple of weeks before. By the summer of 2008, I'd realized that I wasn't happy with Hearthstone and had looked at a few places, but all this, again, without constructing any timelines in my head.

The pushing incident made my decision for me. The options were simplified by the fact that George had apparently been blackballed from all the Hearthstone facilities, including the one in Manhattan. So Eightieth Street was what was left.

George moved into the Eightieth Street Residence, on East Eightieth Street between First Avenue and York, late in September. Is this his last stop? I'd be a fool to predict anything with certainty. But for the time being, I can catch my breath. There's the sense of respite: a harbor, an oasis.

When I began to visit George regularly at Eightieth Street, which was after I began to feel confident he wouldn't make a run for it and try to sprint home, it was late October. Fall happens to be my favorite time of year in New York, and the first

walks we took are still our favorite walks—along the promenade by the East River, near Carl Schurz Park. I think it was
on our very first walk that I noticed some festive event taking
place down in the sports area, where later we would sometimes
see weekend hockey players on rollerblades. This particular event turned out to be a Halloween costume contest for
neighborhood dogs—very Upper East Side. I had foolishly felt,
when I'd visited the Eightieth Street Residence in 2007 and
again in summer 2008, that the place was too fancy, too up-
scale. I had thought that maybe George's being in Westchester County would be an advantage. What on earth had I been
thinking? I hadn't been thinking, of course. I'd been putting
one foot in front of the other.

October, November . . . I always love the shortening of
days in the fall in New York. As the light faded in the afternoons, George's tiny room was a peaceful place to spend an
hour. We'd listen to a CD. He'd lie on his bed, I'd sit in his
armchair and read or correct papers. Sometimes—and this
usually made me cry—I'd lie down next to him and stroke his
hair. Or I'd put my hand on his chest, and he'd put his hand
over mine.

The difficult months and years before I placed George; the
difficult decision to place him; the bumpy months while he
was in White Plains; all this period was—with remarkable
smoothness—relegated to a past, a past which had been full of
challenges but was now behind us. It was as if, instead of struggling like underrehearsed actors in an unwelcome spotlight,
George and I could both, at least for a little while, sit back and
look on. When life sidelines you, you get to be a spectator.
And Carl Schurz Park and the Promenade, and later, the Metropolitan Museum, Central Park, the Frick Collection . . . all
these destinations offered pleasant walks, endless vistas.

Sometime in the 1980s, George wrote a piano piece that he
titled "Suave Mari Magno." These words are the first phrase
of the passage that opens Book II of Lucretius's Latin poem *De*

Rerum Natura. Here is A. E. Stallings's recent translation of the beginning of this passage:

> How sweet it is to watch from dry land when the storm-
>   winds roil
> A mighty ocean's water, and see another's bitter toil—
> Not because you relish someone else's misery—
> Rather, it's sweet to know from what misfortunes you
>   are free.

Perhaps there is a touch of schadenfreude in this notion of a safe haven, removed from the struggles one contemplates below. But there is also a profound truth to the picture. We know how hard to bear the misfortunes are; we ourselves have been tossed in that sea.

In a poem I wrote in late fall, the image that occurred to me was another kind of haven: an oasis. Oases are small and finite; they may even be illusory. But in the meantime, what a relief!

Oasis

The heat and fever over, calmer weather
can prevail. The fumes of smoldering anger

blow back to where they came from,
wherever that was; and the luminous

vacancy they leave behind fills up
with quiet. Why should this be a surprise?

Not far behind the agitation,
plenty of peace had waited for its turn.

"Youth was over," wrote Virginia Woolf
of George Eliot, "but youth had been

full of suffering." To this oasis
(music playing, lamplight on my page)

the roaring world contracts. It's cold outside.
In a while we'll put our hats and coats on

and venture out to stroll beside the river,
November wind, the heat and fever over.

CHAPTER 30

Tithonus

We are far from being ageless, we wives of the residents. Most of us are over sixty, and it shows. Nevertheless, something about visiting our husbands, especially early in the day, when hours of daylight stretch emptily ahead, reminds me of the myth of Eos and Tithonus. The goddess of the dawn (Eos in Greek, Aurora in Latin) fell in love with Tithonus, a handsome young man. She sought and was granted immortality for her lover, but she forgot to ask for eternal youth for him as well. The horrible result was that Tithonus lived on forever, withered and shriveled. Some versions say that Eos turned the old man into a cicada or a grasshopper, creatures the Greeks associated with old age—in the third book of the *Iliad*, Homer compares the voices of the old men on the walls of Troy to the chirping of cicadas. Tithonus, too, in his extreme old age, had only a piping or inaudible voice.

Juxtaposing as it does love and decrepitude, the serene radiance of immortal beauty and the prolonged humiliation of old age, the story of Tithonus has a stark power that has long attracted lyric poets. A recently discovered fragment of Sappho, lamenting the loss of the poet's youth, cites the story of Tithonus as an example of the inevitability of old age.

> Pursue the beautiful gifts of the violet Muses,
> you children, and the high, song-loving lyre.
>
> My skin was soft before, but now old age
> claims it; my hair's gone from black to white.

My spirit has grown heavy; knees can't hold me,
though once they could dance, light as fawns.

I often groan, but what can I do?
Being an ageless human is not possible.

For they say rosy-armed Dawn in love
went to the ends of earth holding Tithonos,

beautiful and young, but in time grey old age
seized him too, even with an immortal wife.

(translated by Diane Rayor)

The fullest ancient treatment of the story is found in the *Homeric Hymn to Aphrodite*, in which the goddess of love, smitten with the mortal Anchises and indeed pregnant by him, uses the story of Eos and Tithonus as a cautionary tale; she will not do to Anchises what Eos unwittingly did to Tithonus.

So, too, golden-throned Eos abducted Tithonus,
one of your own race, who resembled the immortals.
She went to ask Kronion, lord of dark clouds,
that he should be immortal and live forever.
And Zeus nodded assent to her and fulfilled her wish.
Mighty Eos was too foolish to think of asking
youth for him and to strip him of baneful old age.
Indeed, so long as much-coveted youth was his,
he took his delight in early-born, golden-throned Eos,
and dwelt by the stream of Okeanos at the ends of the earth.
But when the first gray hairs began to flow down
from his comely head and noble chin,
mighty Eos did refrain from his bed,
though she kept him in her house and pampered him
with food and ambrosia and gifts of fine clothing.
But when detested old age weighed heavy on him
and he could move or lift none of his limbs,
this is the counsel that to her seemed best in her heart:
she placed him in a chamber and shut its shining doors.

(translated by Apostolos Athanassakis)

In this haunting story, two details are especially striking—one major, part of the very fabric of the myth; one minor, and more, though not entirely, a matter of translation. First is the fact that Eos is not only immortal, being a goddess; she is the goddess of dawn, endlessly youthful and dewy, reborn to radiance each day—a reminder that although mortals age and die, the natural world endlessly recreates itself afresh.

Second is the grim problem of what to do with the eternally aging Tithonus. The Homeric Hymn minces no words. As long as he is youthful and attractive, Eos shares his bed. When he begins to show signs of age, she no longer sleeps with him, but she still lives with him, and she "pampered him / with food and ambrosia and gifts of fine clothing." Finally, though, faced with a very old man, the goddess of dawn opts, as so many consorts do, for placement. This is how Chapman (1559?–1634) describes it in his translation:

> Her counsaíle then thought best to strive no more,
> But lay him in his bed and lock his Dore.

In Athanassakis's translation, however, the verb is precisely the one with whose special use I have become familiar over the years: "she placed him in a chamber and shut its shining doors." She is responsible for him, she has to shelter him, but whether or not she still allows him to live with her (it is not clear where the "chamber" is), she doesn't want to be confronted with him every day.

So where is Tithonus's eternity of decrepitude spent? In a bedroom? I picture some kind of institution, perhaps an old-age home in the sky. It's harder to imagine that this existence is to last forever.

In the sonorously beautiful poem "Tithonus," Tennyson's eponymous speaker refers to himself as "A white-hair'd shadow roaming like a dream / The ever-silent spaces of the East, / Far-folded mists, and gleaming halls of morn." More chilling, A. E. Stallings's poem "Tithonus" locates the old man not, as Tennyson does, "wither[ing] slowly" in the arms of Dawn, but seated in a chair, presumably too weak to walk, visited by Dawn, who then must go away.

Tithonus

Do not look at me, and let me turn away
When you set me by the window in my chair,
Cover me with blankets, give me breakfast on a tray
(Soon the sky will glow with your red hair),

And I will convince us both that I am gone.
I will mutter nursery rhymes and drool,
Stare blankly as my bath is being drawn.
(You bathe my hollowed thighs. Your touch is cool.)

I will divert us with my nonsense words,
Forget your arms, the slight twitch of surprise
That I am light as paper, leaves, the eggshell skulls of birds.
(My whole weight in the bulged spheres of my eyes.)

You feed me nectar from a spoon.
You bite your lip. I swallow and you wince.
(Once I too was beautiful.) Soon
You must go. You take my dish to rinse.

I watch as you tread, shining, up the hill,
I watch you as the world does, as I must.
(The landscape is anonymous, and still:
All elements, and minerals, and dust.)

A. E. Stallings, *Archaic Smile*

Stallings's Tithonus is in fact in a place very like a nursing home, and Dawn plays nurse briefly before she departs. The pattern of visit and departure, profoundly true to the world of such institutions, is heartbreaking.

In my own "Tithonus," I borrow both from Stallings and from the recent novel *The Story of Forgetting* (I've already alluded to it), by a very young writer, Stefan Merrill Block. The book is about early-onset dementia, and a detail that stuck with me is that in it, an institution for demented people is called The Waiting Room. Eternally, Tithonus and all the residents in all these institutions wait. We spouses or partners visit our loved ones, as the phrase has it; then we leave. Like the sun, we'll return. Like Tithonus, they wither slowly.

Tithonus

With thanks to Sappho's Tithonus, Tennyson's "Tithonus,"
A. E. Stallings's "Tithonus," and Stefan Merrill Block's *The Story of Forgetting*

Morning again. So what to do all day?
A golden sunbeam touches the TV.
Oh poker-faced potential of the hours
that stretch ahead, the vase of withered flowers
(sunflowers!) I brought—was it last week?
Tithonus greets me, but he doesn't speak.

In the imagination's attic room,
that vast myth kitty, he has sat—how long?—
waiting, apparently, for some occasion.
Is it relevant that Halloween
is coming? Time to put our costumes on.
Neither quite fits. The radiant young wife

(and need I add immortal?): let me play
her part this sunny, crisp October noon.
What if my sixtieth birthday's within reach?
I'm still clinging to the gift of speech.
Tithonus has been staying in his room
sunk in silence like a living tomb.

Eternal Rorschach of Tithonus: husband
Sappho saw as an emblem of our fate,
being human, "whom grey old age in time

overtook." I focus on the long
duration of that gradual withering,
its languid cadence, Tennysonian.

Stallings, closer to where we fit in,
sees Tithonus as a resident
wandering the hallways, sitting down again
in what one novelist too young to know
yet understood and called "The Waiting Room."
Stallings's Tithonus silently

as in dream speaks to his busy wife:
"You feed me nectar from a spoon."
Nectar: ageless and immortal juice,
gods' wine, held out; he opens his dry mouth
and sucks it in like so much medicine.
"You bathe my hollowed thighs. Your touch is cool.

Soon you must go. You take my dish to rinse."
Aurora, who has business in the sky,
is on a cosmic schedule, while I
usually visit in the afternoon—
nothing arduous, and yet I find
I am exhausted by the time I go.

I and my Tithonus: both will die.
And yet the creeping pace, the golden light,
the bond at which we feebly tug and pluck,
love, is that it, grown changeable and pliant . . .
Tithonus stands beside me quietly.
I lean against him when I say goodbye.

We wives have not made Dawn's careless mistake; we didn't
either ask or forget to ask for eternal youth for our husbands.
Nor are we immortal ourselves; many of us may well end up
sitting where our Tithonuses are now. Nevertheless, when we
visit, we seem young and beautiful and strong—if only by

contrast and if only to ourselves. And the logic of the situation forces us to behave with Dawn's heartless briskness, feeding Tithonus, bathing him, rinsing his dish, and, inevitably, leaving.

CHAPTER 31

The Birthday Party

George's birthday, May 11, always falls on or near Mother's Day. This year, 2009, he turns sixty-six on a Monday, so I give a little party for him at the Eightieth Street Residence on Sunday, which is Mother's Day. Early in the afternoon it's sunny, and an unusual number of small children are frolicking on the downstairs patio. "This is your only granddaughter," a young woman says to one of the residents, showing her a baby. Other families, in different generational permutations, drift out to the patio from the living room. By this time, almost eight months into George's residence here, I know many of the people— visitors as well as residents—by sight or by name. Some of the visitors are friendly; some, like most of the residents they have come to see, appear to be in a private zone, acting as if the figures around them were invisible or nonexistent.

Small children can be ice-breakers. When our son was two or three, we took him a few times to the rehabilitation facility where George's mother had moved after her stroke. I remember that as we walked with him through the corridors, heads would turn to look at him like flowers turning toward the sun. In a nursing home, a toddler or a baby is a precious commodity. In this place, maybe not so much—and yet that's not really true. Luz, the social worker, brings her eighteen-month-old daughter in on Saturdays, and I sense that sunlight effect. "She volunteers," says Luz proudly.

The party doesn't start till two. I've arrived early, as usual, so we have plenty of time. George and I stroll out to the promenade that runs by the East River. On our way back, we stop at a Good Humor truck parked on East End Avenue and Eighty-third Street and buy toasted almond popsicles. When I was a child, the Good Humor man used to call these Roastie-Toasties. They're pleasantly crunchy, even if the main flavor is of almond extract. We wait to eat them till we're back in the patio garden. By now most of the visiting families have left—gone out to Mother's Day lunches, perhaps.

We go back up to the ninth floor, where George's room is. He sits down in the dining area to eat the lunch they've saved for him. Alone for a bit in his little room, I go through his chest of drawers, subtracting mateless socks to take home for the rag bag, hanging up a pair of olive-green corduroy slacks in the wardrobe. Lunch done, he and I go out onto the sunny patio. We're lucky he is on this floor; only the ninth floor has a rooftop patio. I spread out my boxes of watercolors on one of the faux wrought-iron tables. Today I've brought three coloring books: one of mandalas and one of birds. The third, which features pictures taken from medieval tapestries, was given to me by Amy, whose father, Sam, moved onto George's floor about a month ago, just around the time I had the happy idea of painting in coloring books during my visits.

If I knew how to knit or embroider or crochet, I could do those things during the quiet time I spend visiting George. If I were Penelope and had a small portable loom, I could weave and then unweave. But these coloring books suit me very well. On and off for a week or two, I've been working on a tricky mandala that features pouting-mouthed goldfish and many small bubbles. I sometimes ask George for advice about colors, and he sometimes gives it—a one-word reply suffices, and he's good at those. "Red!" "Purple!"

The day I first brought the coloring book with birds, he painted a little himself. We chose (he chose? I chose?) a depiction of a cedar waxwing on a hemlock bough. Immediately I remembered Squirrel Island and the cedar waxwings that used to sit on a bough near the side porch of George's mother's cottage. I remembered the fragrant air, the sound of foghorns, the special brightness in the light that you sometimes get near the ocean even when the water is out of sight. "Remember the cedar waxwings at Squirrel Island?" I asked. When George was first living away from home, in the bad place in White Plains, one reason visits were so painful was that I was afraid to mention anything that might remind him of home—the cats, for example. I was afraid he'd say, "I want to go home and see the cats!" So there was almost nothing to talk about—politics? baseball? Now I understand that talking about familiar things is a good idea. Much of what I mention I think he remembers; if he doesn't, that's all right, too.

The day he painted in the bird coloring book, he used bright colors, making the bird's wing orange. Sometimes he was tempted to dip his brush into my coffee, but he painted quite neatly, keeping within the lines. Soon he tired of this activity. The way I tell when he's tired of something is that he stops looking at the TV screen or the coloring book page and turns to look at me.

It's two o'clock now—time for the party to begin. After a longer than usual wait for the elevator, we get back down to the first floor and into the library, a pleasant room with bookshelves and a big table. Paper cups and plates have been set out, and plastic forks. There's a cake stand and a fancy cake knife for the cake I've brought, a red velvet cake with cream cheese icing, "GEORGE" written in azure letters across the top, and a decorative motif of small sugar soccer balls.

One friend from George's former life is already waiting for us in the library. Presently two or three more people from outside drift in. In addition, there are Lenore, whose husband, Bob, also here, is a resident, and Eve, whose husband, Stanley, is sick upstairs today, and that's about it. It's a little strange for this odd assortment of people to be sitting around the library table; we might be at a committee meeting or a family meal. If there were more of us, we could stand up and act as if this were a cocktail party, as happened at the gathering for George's book back in December. Still, as I slice cake and pour wine or soda, all of us except George manage to carry on a desultory conversation. People talk about the color of the cake (I think I remember Bob asking Lenore, "What makes this cake red?"). One guest won't eat it; he says he's phobic. Red Dye Number Two? I ask. Maybe it's beet juice, he offers. Eve tells a complicated story about conducting a concert in Canada in 1978, which was apparently the year Canada officially proclaimed that women were persons. Lenore talks about *God of Carnage*, the Broadway show she has just seen. At last week's support group in this very room, at this table, she told me she was going to see it.

I stand up and excuse myself for a few minutes: I'm going to go back up to the ninth floor to see if I can bring Sam down to the party. Lenore admires my pants: white slacks with a vivid coiling pattern, part paisley, part snake, in aquamarine and purple, winding up one thigh. The pants turn out to be one leitmotif of the day; like red velvet cake, they seem to be a mild conversation piece.

When I get up to the ninth floor, Sam is asleep, huddled in a comfortable chair on the sunny patio, near the table where earlier in this long day I was painting the fish mandala. I don't want to rouse him, so I go back downstairs. The party is in—I wouldn't exactly call it full swing, but a bit of social energy survives. The afternoon is still sunny, so we move outside to the patio and sit for a little while around a picnic table with an umbrella. I'm between George and Bob. Bob is turned toward his wife, which means he's turned away from me; realizing this, he apologizes. Lenore murmurs, "It's funny how manners stay, isn't it?" George and I offer Bob a cigarette, which pleases him but then proves puzzling. "I don't know how to smoke it," he says to Lenore.

Readjustments: now I am between George and Eve. Eve is talking about financial matters. Another visitor from outside has arrived, and is talking, also about finance, I think—I'm not really listening. George is beginning to get tired; that is, he's turning toward me. Not that he was looking at anyone in particular earlier, but he laughed when laughter was appropriate. Now he looks—what? It's not always easy to tell under his beard. Wistful? Somber? Urgent? Bushy brown beard with some gray and red; pale blue eyes—something Melvillean? Certainly nineteenth century.

Time to go back upstairs. George carries his birthday presents—a big black Mets T-shirt and a box of chocolates—and the bag with wine to the elevator; I have a slice of cake to take upstairs to Sam. Back on nine, we find Sam sitting on the sofa in the living room area, watching TV. I sit at the table with him while he eats the cake; George wanders out onto the patio for a cigarette. Sam is always courtly and pleasant. He is hard of hearing and has very little short-term memory, but if you work around these disabilities, it is perfectly possible to carry on a conversation. He's reluctant to eat the cake when no one else is having any, so I explain to him that everyone else has already had theirs. He missed the party downstairs because he was napping out on the patio.

"I was out there in the sun," he says. "It was pleasant. I was thinking about Milton. 'Yet once more, O ye laurels . . .'" and he proceeds to quote with total accuracy the first five lines of *Lycidas*. I have a feeling he could go on. I say the last line with him: "Shatter your leaves before the mellowing year."

"Last year was a big Milton year," I tell him. "It was Milton's four hundredth birthday."

I go out on the patio to see what George is doing, which isn't much. I go back to his room to get the bottle of bubble stuff I keep on his dresser. We blow some bubbles over the bars that prevent anyone from falling or jumping off the patio; they spin away in the wind, up into the sky or west toward First

Avenue. Years and years ago, we used to blow bubbles in Riverside Park with Jonathan; "bubble" was one of his first words. In Vermont, in the days when he smoked a pipe, George used to blow smoke-filled bubbles, which were heavy and cloudy and released magical puffs of smoke when they burst.

George tries to catch some of the bubbles we're blowing, and laughs. Other bubbles land with a silent plop on the pages of the coloring book I've brought out again with the paints, brushes, and a glass of water. I've just about finished the fish mandala, and for a change of pace I open the medieval tapestry coloring book Amy passed on to me. I choose a picture of Death riding a pale horse. I think I'll paint the sky an ominous, apocalyptic red. But for now, I twirl a small brush first in the green paint, then in the yellow, and begin to color in the leaves on the trees of the forest through which Death is riding.

ACKNOWLEDGMENTS

So many people have sustained me since 2005 that naming them is inevitably an exercise in omissions. Nevertheless, I have to name at least a handful. My son, Jonathan; my sister, Beth, without whom this book might never have been published; and my nephew Edward. In Vermont, Reeve Lindbergh, Nat Tripp, and the Holden family. At Rutgers, my colleagues both in and out of the English Department, especially Fran Bartkowski, Alice Dark, Lynn Mullins, and John Straus. In the poetry world, Lorna Blake, Gardner McFall, Molly Peacock, Michael Snediker, and A. E. Stallings. From support groups, Martie Barylick, Carol Boulanger, and so many others. At the Eightieth Street Residence, the management and staff and all the other spouses. Dr. James Noble, Dr. Barbara Waxenberg, Donna Curcio Luci, and Susan Denenberg. Finally, my publisher, Paul Dry, and his editors Barbara Morrow and John Corenswet, and my patient and stalwart typist, John Heuston. During years when I needed a great deal of help, all these people and more helped me in more ways than I can say. To all, my deep gratitude.

Some of the chapters of this book have been previously published in slightly different form: "Readings in the Kingdom of Illness" in *Literary Imagination*; "Into the Murky World," *Families, Systems, and Health*; "Around the Table," the *Threepenny Review*; "Similes," *Southwest Review*; "Backups," the *Yale*

Review; "Tithonus," *Literary Imagination*; "So Long Without Loving," *New Ohio Review*.

The following poems have been previously published, occasionally in slightly different form or with different titles: "Bath" and "One More Thought," *Neurology Now*; "The Beam," the *New Criterion*; "The Boat" and "The Concert," the *Hudson Review*; "Choice," the *Saint Ann's Review*; "The Coaster," *Southwest Review*; "The Cold Hill Side" and "New Year," the *New Yorker*; "Deplaning," *Agenda*; "Dreams in a Damp House" and "The Stack," *New England Review*; "In the Drawer," *Poetry London*; "In Your Chair," the *New Republic*; "Loneliness," the *Times Literary Supplement*; "Minus" and "Hotel," *First Things*; "Monodrama," *Bellevue Literary Review*; "Push Me Pull You," *Barrow Street*; "Snake," *Raritan*; "Two Silences," *College Hill Review*; "Wiggle Room," *Per Contra*.

These poems appeared in my 2010 book *The Ache of Appetite*: "Choice," "Wiggle Room," "Push Me Pull You," "Monodrama," "Minus," "The Beam," "Loneliness," "The Boat," "The Cold Hill Side," "Hotel," "Snake."

The author and publisher gratefully acknowledge the following additional sources:

W. H. Auden, excerpt from "Good-bye to the Mezzogiorno" from *W. H. Auden: Collected Poems*, edited by Edward Mendelson. Copyright © 1958 by W. H. Auden. Used by permission of Random House, Inc. and The Wylie Agency, Ltd.

C. P. Cavafy, "Walls," translated by Edmund Keeley and Philip Sherrard, from *C. P. Cavafy: Collected Poems*. Copyright © 1975, 1992 by Edmund Keeley and Philip Sherrard. Reprinted by permission of Princeton University Press. Excerpt from "Days of 1964," translated by James Merrill, from *Collected Poems*, edited by J. D. McClatchy and Stephen Yenser. Copyright © 2001 by the Literary Estate of

James Merrill at Washington University. Used by permission of Alfred A. Knopf, a division of Random House, Inc.

Emily Dickinson, "Because I could not stop for Death—" and "Crumbling is not an instant's Act" from *The Poems of Emily Dickinson*, edited by Thomas H. Johnson. Copyright 1951, © 1955, 1979, 1983 by the President and Fellows of Harvard College. All rights reserved. Reprinted by permission of the Belknap Press of Harvard University Press.

Robert Frost, "Home Burial" from *The Poetry of Robert Frost*, edited by Edward Connery Lathem. Copyright 1930, 1939, 1947, © 1969 by Henry Holt and Company. Copyright © 1958 by Robert Frost. Copyright © 1967 by Lesley Frost Ballantine. Reprinted by arrangement with Henry Holt and Company, LLC and Random House (UK) Ltd.

Homer, excerpt from "To Aphrodite," translated by Apostolos Athanassakis, from *The Homeric Hymns* Copyright © 1976, 2004 by The Johns Hopkins University Press. Reprinted with the permission of The Johns Hopkins University Press.

Philip Larkin, "Talking in Bed" from *Philip Larkin: Collected Poems*, edited by Anthony Thwaite. Copyright © 1988 by the Estate of Philip Larkin. Reprinted by permission of Farrar, Straus & Giroux, LLC and Faber and Faber Ltd. "As Bad as a Mile" from *The Whitsun Weddings*. Copyright © 1964 by Philip Larkin. Reprinted by permission of Farrar, Straus & Giroux, LLC and Faber & Faber, Ltd.

Lucretius, excerpt from Part II from "De Rerum Natura," translated by A. E. Stallings, from *The Nature of Things* (Penguin Classics). Reprinted with the permission of the translator.

James Merrill, excerpt from "Manitees" from *Collected Poems*. Copyright © 2001 by the Literary Estate of James Merrill at Washington University. Used by permission of Alfred A. Knopf, a division of Random House, Inc.